Hampton-Brown ▶EDGE

Acknowledgments

Grateful acknowledgment is given to the authors, artists, photographers, museums, publishers, and agents for permission to reprint copyrighted material. Every effort has been made to secure the appropriate permission. If any omissions have been made or if corrections are required, please contact the Publisher.

Photographic Credits

Cover: The "Unisphere" Sculpture Celebrates Humanity's Interdependence, Queens, New York, USA, James P. Blair. Photograph © James P. Blair/National Geographic Stock. **1** ©Frank Romero; ©Image Source/Alamy. **2** ©Olinchuk/Shutterstock. **3** ©JUPITERIMAGES/BananaStock/Alamy. **6** ©Steve Sant/Alamy; ©JUPITERIMAGES/Brand X/Alamy. **10** ©Glow Images/Alamy. **12** ©Modricker/Corbis. **13** ©Bonnie Kamin/PhotoEdit Inc. **14** ©fotoluminate/Shutterstock. **15** (l) ©fotomine/Shutterstock; (r) ©1000 Words/Shutterstock. **16** ©Myrleen Ferguson Cate/PhotoEdit Inc. **17** ©Paul Burns/Lifesize/Getty Images: ©Comstock Images/jupiterimages; ©Sean Justice/Getty Images. **19** ©Jeff Greenberg/PhotoEdit. **20** ©Bob Daemmrich/PhotoEdit. **21** ©Bill Bachmann/PhotoEdit. **22** ©Michael Newman/PhotoEdit. **24** ©Anthony Marsland/The Image Banks/Getty Images. **34** © Ilene MacDonald/Alamy. **35** ©oliveromg/Shutterstock. **36** ©Digital Vision/Alamy. **38** ©Ariel Skelley/Getty Images/Blend Images. **39** ©JUPITERIMAGES/Polka Dot/Alamy. **43** ©PhotoDisc/PunchStock. **44** ©Comstock Images/jupiterimages. **45** ©Polka Dot/PunchStock. **46** ©Masterfile/Radious Images/Alamy. **49** ©Thinkstock/PunchStock. **52** ©Bill Stormont/Corbis. **54** ©Redmond Durrell/Alalmy; ©Alan Carey/Corbis. **55** ©PhotoDisc/PunchStock. **67** ©Karina Wang/Getty Images. **68** ©Gary Crabbe /Alamy. **69** (l) ©Ron Chapple/Corbis; (r) ©Atlantide Phototravel/Corbis. **71** ©Nicolas Russell/The Image Bank/Getty Images; ©Photofusion Picture Library/Alamy. **72** ©Jeff Greenberg/Alamy; ©Sean Justice/Corbis. **76** ©Somos Images LLC/Alamy. **77** ©Tom Carter/PhotoEdit. **78** ©Ilene MacDonald/Alamy. **80** ©Comstock/jupiterimages. **81** ©Rubberball/Alamy. **85** ©JUPITERIMAGES/BananaStock/Alamy. **86** ©JUPITERIMAGES/Comstock Images/Alamy. **87** ©Bob Daemmrich/PhotoEdit. **89** ©Terrance Klassen/Alamy. **105** ©Marko Georgiev/Getty Images. **142** ©moodboard/Alamy. **146** ©Design Pics Inc./Alamy.

For product information and technology asistance, contact us at **Cengage Learning Customer & Sales Support, 1-800-354-9706**

For permission to use material from this text or product, submit all requests online at **www.cengage.com/permissions** Further permissions questions can be emailed to **permissionrequest@cengage.com**

National Geographic Learning | Cengage Learning
1 Lower Ragsdale Drive
Building 1, Suite 200
Monterey, CA 93940

Cengage Learning is a leading provider of customized learning solutions with office locations around the globe, including Singapore, the United Kingdom, Australia, Mexico, Brazil, and Japan. Locate your local office at **www.cengage.com/global**.

Visit National Geographic Learning online at **ngl.cengage.com**
Visit our corporate website at **www.cengage.com**

B and B, Newburyport, MA

ISBN: 978-1-285-73569-6 (Practice Book)
ISBN: 978-1-285-73570-2 (Practice Book Teacher's Annotated Edition)

ISBN: 978-1-285-76734-5 (Practice Masters)
Teachers are authorized to reproduce the practice masters in this book in limited quantity and solely for use in their own classrooms.

Printed in the United States of America

13 22

Contents

Contents, *continued*

UNIT 2

Grammar

✔ Edit and Proofread

Grammar Review

UNIT 3

Grammar

✔ Edit and Proofread

Grammar Review

Contents, *continued*

UNIT 4

Grammar

✔ Edit and Proofread

Grammar Review

UNIT 5

Grammar

✔ Edit and Proofread

Grammar Review

Contents, *continued*

Use the Verb *Be*

The verb **be** has three forms: **am**, **is**, and **are**. Use these verbs to tell about yourself and others.

Who	Use	Example	Who	Use	Example
yourself	**I + am**	**I am** Maya.	yourself and another person	**we + are**	Rosa and I are sisters. **We are** from Mexico.
someone you speak to	**you + are**	**You are** a visitor.	two or more people you speak to	**you + are**	**You are** visitors.
one other person	**he + is** **she + is**	Juan is tall. **He is** my brother. Rosa is my big sister. **She is** seventeen.	two or more people or things	**they + are**	My parents are good people. **They are** hard workers.
one thing	**it + is**	Our home is busy. **It is** a happy place.			

Try It

A. Complete each sentence about the family. Write the correct form of the verb.

1. I _____ Mama's helper.
   am / are

2. She _____ also Maya.
   is / are

3. Juan _____ Mama's helper, too.
   am / is

4. He works with Rosa. They _____ good workers.
   is / are

B. Complete each sentence about little Carlos. Use am, is, or are.

5. Carlos _____ my younger brother.

6. Carlos plays with trucks. They _____ his favorite toys.

7. Carlos likes to tell jokes. He _____ funny.

8. I _____ happy he is my brother.

① Make a Statement

- A **statement** tells something. Like all sentences, it has a **subject** and a **predicate**. It ends with a period.

  <u>Names of some states</u> <u>are</u> names of people.

  <u>I</u> <u>am</u> from Georgia in the United States.

  <u>Georgia</u> <u>is</u> a name from King George II of England.

- A predicate always has a <u>**verb**</u>.

- In a statement, the subject usually comes before the verb.

Georgia is the name of a state.

Try It

A. Put the words in the right order to make a statement. Write the statement correctly. Use a period.

1. am / from the state of Washington / I / . _____

2. from George Washington / is / The name / . _____
_____

3. Virginia / the name of a state / is / . _____

4. is / the name of my best friend / It / . _____

5. in the same class at school / We / are / . _____

B. Draw a line from each subject to the correct predicate.

6. Other names	is also the name of my cousin.
7. Alabama	are names of states, too.
8. It	is the name of a dessert and a state.
9. Alaska	are happy to learn about other names.
10. We	is a state next to Georgia.

2 Ask a Question

> • A **question** asks something. Like all sentences, it has a **subject** and a **predicate**. It ends with a question mark.
>
> > **Am I happy with the name Ramón?**
> >
> > **Is Elizabeth happy with her name?**
> >
> > **Is Liz the short form of her name?**
>
> • In a question, the **verb** comes before the subject.

Is Ramón a common name?

Try It

A. Put the words in the right order to ask a question. Write the question correctly. Use a question mark.

1. my grandparents / nice people / Are / ? _____

2. Is / happy with the name Henry / Grandpa / ? _____
   _____

3. happy with the name Henrietta / Grandma / Is / ? _____
   _____

4. it / strange to have similar names / Is / ? _____

5. the friend of a Henry or Henrietta / Are / you / ? _____
   _____

B. Read each statement. Then write it as a question.

6. Ramón is my cousin. _____

7. We are happy with our names. _____

8. He is proud of his last name. _____

9. Names like Gonzales are great. _____

10. I am glad to know the Gonzales family. _____

③ Make a Negative Statement

- The word **not** is a **negative word**. A statement with the word **not** is a negative statement.
- In a statement, **not** comes after the **verbs am**, **is**, and **are**.

Statement	Negative Statement
My cousins **are** happy with their names.	My cousins **are** **not** happy with their names.
Tiny **is** a good name for a dog.	Tiny **is** **not** a good name for a dog.
I **am** ready to change my name.	I **am** **not** ready to change my name.

Try It

A. Add the word **not** to make each statement negative. Write the negative statement.

1. Alexander is eager to change his name. _____

_____

2. I am in need of a new name. _____

3. Short names are good. _____

4. Alexander is happy with the name Al. _____

5. We are ready for his new name. _____

B. Rewrite each statement about names to make it negative. Add the word **not**.

6. My name is Collin. _____

7. Siegfried and Sigmund are funny names. _____

_____

8. I am in a hurry to change names. _____

4 Use a Contraction

- A **contraction** is a shorter way to say two words.
- You can join a **verb** and **not** to form a contraction. Use an apostrophe (') to take the place of the letter you leave out.

1. My cat's name **is not** Inky.

   My cat's name **isn't** Inky.

2. Cats **are not** easy to find.

   Cats **aren't** easy to find.

Try It

A. Make a contraction from the words in parentheses. Write the correct contraction.

1. We _____ able to find Inky. **(are not)**

2. Inky _____ in the kitchen. **(is not)**

3. She _____ under Jason's bed. **(is not)**

4. "You _____ much help," Jason says. **(are not)**

5. "It _____ an easy job," I say. **(is not)**

B. Use **isn't** or **aren't** to complete each sentence.

6. Names _____ a problem for Jason.
   isn't / aren't

7. He _____ slow to name cats.
   isn't / aren't

8. Our new kitten is playful. Sleepy _____ a good name
   isn't / aren't
   for our kitten.

9. We _____ happy with that name, either.
   isn't / aren't

10. She _____ a sleepy cat. Flash is a better name.
    isn't / aren't

⑤ Learn About Nouns

- A **noun** names a person, place, or thing.
- A **singular noun** names one person, place, or thing.
- A **plural noun** names more than one person, place, or thing.
- To make most nouns plural, just add **-s**.

One	More Than One
river	rivers
cloud	clouds
tree	trees
forest	forests

tulip

tulips

Try It

A. Complete the chart. Write the plural form of each noun.

One	More Than One
1. boy	
2. book	
3. name	
4. field	
5. eagle	
6. sunflower	

B. (7–10) Complete this story. Use plural nouns from the chart.

Mr. Williams is our neighbor. He is a reader of _____. He likes birds. He reads about _____. He also has a garden. There are big _____ in the garden. He has two _____.

6 Use Nouns in the Subject

- A sentence has two parts: a **subject** and a **predicate**. To find the subject, ask, "**Whom** or **what** is the sentence about?"

    The rice is from a new market.

- In many sentences, the subject is a **noun**. Remember, a noun names a person, place, or thing.

    Lee Market is a new store.   **Mr. Lee** is the owner.

    His daughters are good helpers.   **The Lees** are my neighbors.

Try It

A. Complete each subject. Use a noun from the box.

Hannah	Johnstown	mother	store	vegetables

1. _____ is the home of Lee Market.

2. _____ is Mr. Lee's daughter. She is at the store every afternoon.

3. The _____ is always full of people.

4. My _____ is there every day.

5. Fresh _____ are on the shelves.

B. Tell more about this family. Add a noun to complete the subject of each sentence.

6. _____ is the owner of a flower shop on Oak Street.

7. _____ is near Lee Market.

8. _____ is the name of the shop.

9. Mrs. Lee's _____ are helpers in both stores.

10. This _____ is always ready with flowers.

Use Complete Sentences

- A complete sentence has two parts: a **subject** and a **predicate**. The **subject** tells whom or what the sentence is about—or who does the action.

    Mei is a new student. **Luisa and I** are in her math class.

    I am also in her science class.

- The **predicate** tells more about the subject. A predicate always has a **verb**. The verb has to agree with the subject.

Subject	Verb	Example
I	am	**I am** from Colombia.
You	are	**You are** from Colombia, too.
He She It	is	**He is** from Florida. **She is** on our volleyball team. **It is** a great team.
We	are	**We are** happy at our school.
You	are	**You are** both in this class.
They	are	**They are** in this class, too.

Try It

A. Choose a word from the box to complete each sentence.

You	is	are	classmate

1. Lincoln _____ in class with Mei and me.

2. My new _____ is from Illinois, like President Lincoln.

3. "You _____ a friendly person," I tell Lincoln.

4. "_____ are, too," says Lincoln.

B. Draw a line from each subject to the correct predicate.

5. I   is the name of a poet.

6. Walt Whitman   are names of poets, too.

7. My sisters   am Walt.

8. Their names   are happy with our names.

9. We   is an important thing in our family.

10. Poetry   are Emily and Edna.

C. (11–16) Complete this story. Use is or are.

My brother _____ Simón. You _____ Simón, too. Simón _____ a name from Colombia's history. My brother and I _____ in the same history class. We _____ with Luisa in math class. She _____ very smart.

D. Use am, is, or are to complete each sentence.

17. I _____ from South America.

               am / is / are

18. Soccer _____ a big sport there, too.

                    am / is / are

19. My friends _____ at every soccer game.

                     am / is / are

20. A soccer game _____ a lot of fun to watch.

                       am / is / are

21. My brother _____ a soccer coach.

                    am / is / are

22. You _____ in class with him.

               am / is / are

23. Now we _____ ready to play.

               am / is / are

24. You _____ welcome to join us.

               am / is / are

Use the Verb *Do*

The verb **do** has two forms: **do** and **does**.

- Use **do** with **I**, **you**, **we**, or **they**.
- Use **does** with **he**, **she**, or **it**.

Many questions start with **Do** or **Does**. The **subject** comes next, followed by another **verb**.

Question	Answer
Do you like Chicago?	Yes, **I do**.
Does it seem different to you?	No, **it does** not.
Do we have time to see your parents?	Yes, **we do**.
Do they speak English well?	No, **they do** not.

When you answer, use the same verb that starts the sentence. Say the **subject** first and then the verb.

Do you speak Spanish? Yes, **I do**.

Try It

A. Put the words in the right order to ask a question with **do** or **does**. Write the question correctly. Use a question mark.

1. talk to your parents about Mexico / you / Do / ?

_____

2. cook / Mexican food for the family / Do / they / ?

_____

3. Mexican food / you / Do / like / ? _____

B. Complete each question. Use **do** or **does**. Then answer the questions.

4. _____ I like Mexican food? Yes, _____ .

5. _____ it taste spicy? No, _____ .

7 Use Contractions: *Don't* and *Doesn't*

- A **contraction** is a shorter way to say two words. You can join a **verb** and the word **not** to form a contraction. Use an apostrophe (') to take the place of the letter you leave out.

   1. Joe **does not** sing in the choir. | **2.** We **do not** sing, either.

   Joe **doesn't** sing in the choir. | We **don't** sing, either.

- Use the contractions **doesn't** and **don't** to answer questions.

   3. **Does** your brother play ball with you, Joe? | **4.** **Do** you run with your sister?

   No, he **doesn't**. | No, I **don't**.

Try It

A. Answer each question. Make a contraction from the words in parentheses.

   1. Do you come from the Philippines, Joe? No, I _____ . **(do not)**

   2. Do your parents work downtown? No, they _____ . **(do not)**

   3. Does your mother give you piano lessons? No, she _____ . **(does not)**

   4. Does piano music interest you? No, it _____ . **(does not)**

   5. Do we like the same things as you? No, you _____ . **(do not)**

B. Complete an answer to each question. Add a subject and **doesn't** or **don't**.

   6. Do you paint pictures, Soon-Jin? No, _____ .

   7. Does your father like art? No, _____ .

   8. Does art seem like fun to you? No, _____ .

   9. Do your cousins make artwork? No, _____ .

   10. Does your sister go to art school? No, _____ .

8 Ask Questions with *Do*

- You can use **do** to ask questions. Use **do** with **I, you, we,** and **they**. Also use **do** with **plural nouns**.

    Do you have pictures of your family?

    Do we like our family pictures?

    Do they tell about our lives?

- When you ask questions with **do**, the **subject** comes after **do** and before another **verb**.

    Do my **sisters** <u>look</u> like my grandfather?

Do I look like my grandfather?

Try It

A. Put the words in the right order to ask a question with **do**. Write the question correctly.

1. you / Do / have a picture of your cousins / ? _____
   _____

2. live in Argentina / they / Do / ? _____

3. Do / I / the name of their city / know / ? _____

4. send / you / Do / them pictures / ? _____

5. we / share pictures / Do / ? _____

B. Complete each question. Add **do** and another verb.

6. _____ you _____ the people in this picture?

7. _____ they _____ like your mother's family?

8. _____ I _____ pictures of my family?

9. _____ we _____ to look at more pictures?

10. _____ you _____ new pictures of your family?

⑨ Ask Questions with *Does*

- You can use **does** to ask questions. Use **does** with **he**, **she**, and **it**. Also use **does** with **singular nouns**.

  Does Rosa write letters often?

  Does she tell about her brother?

  Does he play basketball?

  Does it seem like a fun game?

- When you ask a question with **does**, the **subject** comes after **does** and before another **verb**.

  Does she <u>write</u> about her classes?

Try It

A. Put the words in the right order to ask a question with does. Write the question correctly.

1. write to her uncle in Egypt / Does / she / ? _____

2. Does / seem like a strange place / it / ? _____

3. Does / write back to her / he / ? _____

4. Does / pictures / send / he / ? _____

5. she / e-mail to him, too / send / Does / ? _____

B. Complete each question. Add does and another verb.

6. _____ she _____ to her grandfather in Peru?

7. _____ he _____ funny stories in each letter?

8. _____ it _____ good to hear from him?

9. _____ she _____ about life at school?

10. _____ he _____ to visit the United States?

⑩ Use Pronouns: *He* and *She*

- A **noun** names a person, place, or thing. A noun can be the subject of a sentence.

    Hiro plays baseball. **Jen** has pen pals.

- A **pronoun** refers to a noun. It can be the **subject** of a sentence, too.

    He plays baseball. **She** has pen pals.

- Use the pronoun **he** to talk about one boy or one man.

    Hiro lives in Japan. **He** is in high school.

- Use the pronoun **she** to talk about one girl or one woman.

    Jen lives in the United States. **She** plays soccer.

- Should you use **he** or **she**? Look at an earlier sentence. Find the **noun** that **he** or **she** goes with.

    Hiro likes sports, too. **He** plays well.

    His **aunt** teaches at our school. **She** often talks about Hiro.

Try It

A. Use **he** or **she** to finish the sentence pairs. Underline the noun that **he** or **she** goes with.

1. Hiro is a good catcher. _____ is part of a great team.

2. Hiro's grandmother loves baseball. _____ goes to every game.

3. Jen is the goalie on the soccer team. _____ stops almost every ball.

B. (4–6) Complete this story about Hiro and Jen. Add **he** or **she**.

Jen writes to Hiro every week. _____ tells about her life. Hiro writes

back. _____ asks about sports. Jen gives the scores of her games.

_____ is proud of her team.

11 Use Pronouns: *It* and *They*

- A **noun**—a person, place, or thing—can be the **subject** of a sentence. A **pronoun** can refer to a noun.

- Use the pronoun **it** to talk about one thing or one place.

  > **Dallas** is my home. **It** is my favorite place.

  > Our **garden** is small. **It** is in front of our building.

- Use the pronoun **they** to talk about more than one thing or more than one person.

  > The **plants** are small. **They** grow quickly, though.

  > The **Murrays** live nearby. **They** have a bigger garden.

Try It

A. Use **it** or **they** to finish the sentence pairs. Underline the noun that **it** or **they** goes with.

1. Roses grow well in our garden. _____ have a sweet smell.

2. This plant does not have a smell. _____ grows well in dry places.

3. The Murrays grow flowers and vegetables. _____ often give us vegetables.

4. One tomato is really big. _____ weighs almost two pounds.

5. Fresh flowers are a gift for Mrs. Murray. _____ always make her smile.

B. (6–10) Look at the photos. Then finish this story. Add **it** or **they**.

   The Murrays love their garden. _____ spend many hours there each week. Their garden has a lot of flowers. _____ is a special garden. The garden also has a long path. _____ is made with bricks. Our flowers are pretty. _____ need water and sunlight to grow. I like to take care of our garden. _____ is a beautiful garden.

⑫ Answer a Question with the Right Pronoun

When you answer a question, use the right **pronoun** for the **noun**.

Use	To Tell About	Example
he	one boy or one man	Does your **father** talk about Ethiopia? Yes, **he** does.
she	one girl or one woman	Is your **mother** going to Ethiopia soon? No, **she** is not.
it	one thing or one place	Is this **picture** new? No, **it** is not.
they	more than one thing or more than one person	Do your brothers like to wear a tie? Yes, **they** do.

Try It

A. Draw a line from each question to the correct answer.

1. Do Ayana's relatives come from Ethiopia?   No, it is not.

2. Does Dad have a story about his life there?   Yes, they do.

3. Is the story funny?   Yes, he does.

B. Tell more about Ayana's family. Answer each question. Use the right pronoun.

4. Does Ayana want more facts about her family? _____

5. Is her brother happy to help her? _____

6. Are her cousins part of this project? _____

Use Subject Pronouns

- A **pronoun** takes the place of a noun. A pronoun can be the subject of a sentence. Use the pronoun that goes with the subject.

he   she   it   they

Use	To Tell About	Example
she	one female	**Mrs. Chan** has a nice garden. **She** grows vegetables there with her sons.
he	one male	**Toshiro** helps in the garden. **He** is a friend.
it	one thing	The **rake** is new. **It** is very useful.
they	more than one person or thing	The **Chan brothers** eat well. **They** love fresh vegetables.

- When you answer a question, use the pronoun that matches the subject.

  Does **Mr. Chan** help? Yes, **he** does. Is the **work** hard? No, **it** isn't.

Try It

A. Draw a line from each sentence to the sentence that matches it. Choose the correct pronoun.

1. **Toshiro** picks up a rake.

2. **Weeds** are in the garden.

3. The **garden** needs water.

4. **Mrs. Chan** smiles.

5. **Corn** grows in the garden.

It is dry.

He rakes the garden carefully.

It is part of dinner.

She likes the garden very much.

Now **they** are in the trash.

B. Use the correct pronoun to complete each sentence.

6. Mr. Chan works in a bank. _____ likes the job.
   He / She

7. The bank is downtown. _____ is in a big building.
   He / It

8. The boys visit the bank. _____ meet Mr. Chan for lunch.
   He / They

9. The restaurant is next to the bank. _____ is a good restaurant.
   She / It

10. Mrs. Chan comes to the restaurant, too. _____ likes the food there.
    She / They

11. Mr. Chan pays the bill. _____ thanks the waitress.
    He / It

12. The Chans like Miami. _____ are happy there!
    It / They

C. Use **he**, **she**, **it**, or **they** to answer each question.

13. Do the boys come from Miami? No, _____ don't.

14. Is Mrs. Chan new to Miami? Yes, _____ is.

15. Are both parents from China? Yes, _____ are.

16. Is it easy to move to a new place? No, _____ isn't.

17. Does Mr. Chan miss his old home? No, _____ doesn't.

18. Does Miami feel like home to the Chan family now? Yes, _____ does.

D. Draw a line from each question to the answer that matches it. Choose the correct pronoun.

19. Are the boys at work in the garden?	No, it doesn't.
20. Does that cucumber look ripe?	Yes, they do.
21. Is Mr. Chan in the kitchen?	Yes, he does.
22. Does he help Mrs. Chan cook dinner?	No, she isn't.
23. Is Mrs. Chan ready to eat yet?	Yes, they are.
24. Do the Chans enjoy dinnertime?	Yes, he is.

Use the Verb *Have*

The verb **have** has two forms: **have** and **has**.

- Use **have** with **I**, **you**, **we**, or **they**.
- Use **has** with **he**, **she**, or **it**.

See how these **verbs** agree, or go, with their **subjects**.

I have a family with many talents.

Francisco has a talent for painting.

Our parents have an interest in all the arts.

My mother has a love of music.

Francisco and my mother have a good sense of humor, too.

Try It

A. Complete each sentence. Write the correct form of the verb.

1. Francisco _____ great artwork.
   have / has

2. His paintings _____ trees and flowers.
   have / has

3. "You _____ a great future in art," Dad tells Francisco.
   have / has

4. Dad _____ a big garden.
   have / has

5. His vegetables _____ bright colors and a fresh taste.
   have / has

B. (6–10) Complete this story. Use have or has.

My sister Julia _____ dance lessons every week. Those students

_____ many exercises. Andrea _____ the best form. Her

steps _____ grace. Her teachers say, "We _____ great hopes

for Andrea."

13 Ask a Question

- You can use **do** or **does** with the **verb have** to ask a question.

  > **Do** the girls **have** nice voices? **Does** Consuelo **have** a nice voice?

- The first word in this kind of question is **Do** or **Does**. The next word is the **subject** of the sentence. The verb **have** comes next.

  > **Does Consuelo have** short hair?

- Is the answer "Yes"? Then change **have** to **has** if the subject is one person or **he**, **she**, or **it**.

Question	Answer
Does Consuelo have short hair?	Yes, **Consuelo has** short hair.
Does she have a nice voice?	Yes, **she has** a nice voice.

Try It

A. Put the words in the correct order to ask a question. Write the question. Then write an answer that begins with **Yes**.

1. Consuelo / have dark hair / Does / ? _____

_____

2. great music / Do / have / the singers / ? _____

_____

B. Use **do** or **does** and **have** to complete each question about the concert. Then write an answer.

3. _____ the singers _____ long skirts? Yes, _____

_____.

4. _____ Consuelo _____ a strong voice? Yes, _____

_____.

14 Make a Negative Statement

- A question can begin with **Do** or **Does**. The **subject** of the sentence comes next. The **verb have** follows the subject.

    Do they have new costumes?

    Does Ms. Evans have the script?

- Is the answer "No"? Then put the word **not** between **do** or **does** and **have**.

Question	Answer
Does the boy have a tall hat?	No, **the boy does not have** a tall hat.
Do the students have scripts in their hands?	No, **the students do not have** scripts in their hands.

Try It

A. Answer each question about the photo. Use **do not have** or **does not have**.

1. Does the girl have light hair? No, _____.

2. Does she have a heavy coat? No, _____.

3. Do the students have funny masks? No, _____.

4. Do they have much time for practice? No, _____

    _____.

B. Write one more question and answer about the students in the photo.
Use **do have** or **does have** in your question. Use **No** and **not** in your answer.

5. **Question:** _____

    _____

6. **Answer:** _____

    _____

15 Use Pronouns: *I*, *We*, and *You*

- Use the pronoun **I** to talk about yourself.

  I like this spinach salad.

- Use the pronoun **we** to talk about yourself and another person.

  Beth and I eat vegetables. **We** are healthy eaters.

- Use the pronoun **you** to talk to one or more persons.

  You are always hungry.

Try It

A. Complete each sentence. Write the correct pronoun.

1. My name is Danilo. _____ have lunch with my friends.

I / We

2. My friends and I choose healthy foods. _____ often eat fruit.

I / We

3. Ms. Siegel sees our plates. "_____ are smart eaters!" she says.

We / You

4. My favorite drink is milk. _____ like it a lot.

I / You

5. "Danilo, _____ are full of milk," my friend Jaya laughs.

I / you

B. Complete each sentence. Write **I**, **we**, or **you**.

6. Jaya and I talk together. _____ both eat slowly.

7. "Danilo, _____ are a good friend," Jaya says.

8. _____ share an orange with Jaya.

9. _____ both like oranges.

10. _____ and I eat to stay healthy," I tell Jaya.

16 Use Pronouns in the Subject: *I, You, He, She, It*

Every sentence has a **subject**. To find it, ask yourself: Whom or what is the sentence about?

- The **subject** can be a **noun** or a **pronoun**.

  My uncle teaches many classes. **He** is a great teacher.

Use the correct pronoun:

- If the subject is a boy or a man, use **he**.
- If the subject is a girl or a woman, use **she**.
- If the subject is a place or a thing, use **it**.

Subject Pronouns
Singular
I
you
he, she, it

Try It

A. Change the underlined word or words to the correct pronoun. Write the pronoun.

1. <u>Mr. Silva</u> is my teacher. _____ teaches art.

2. <u>Meg</u> loves art class. _____ paints a picture of a horse.

3. <u>One horse</u> gallops. _____ has long legs.

4. <u>Greg</u> paints pictures, too. _____ uses bright colors.

5. <u>A boat</u> is in the scene. _____ is red and blue.

B. Complete each sentence pair. Use a subject pronoun from the chart.

6. Art class meets after lunch. _____ is a lot of fun.

7. Marie sits by the window. _____ paints a new picture.

8. Mr. Silva walks around the room. _____ helps each student.

9. Marie stands up. _____ is done with the picture.

10. The picture is great! _____ looks just like Marie.

17 Use Pronouns in the Subject

Every sentence has a **subject**. To find it, ask yourself: Whom or what is the sentence about?

- The subject can be a **noun** or a **pronoun**.

  These brothers have many talents. **They** make wonderful music.

Use the correct pronoun:

- If the subject is a boy or a man, use **he**.
- If the subject is a girl or a woman, use **she**.
- If the subject is a place or a thing, use **it**.
- If the subject names more than one person, place, or thing, use **they**.

Subject Pronouns	
Singular	**Plural**
I	we
you	you
he, she, it	they

Try It

A. Change the underlined word or words to the correct pronoun. Write the pronoun in the second sentence of each pair.

1. <u>One brother</u> has light hair. _____ writes the words.

2. <u>The words</u> are funny. _____ make people laugh.

3. <u>The other brother</u> has dark hair. _____ writes the music for the songs.

4. <u>Grandma</u> loves the songs. _____ laughs at the words.

5. <u>The brothers</u> work on a new song each week. _____ want to make an album of their songs.

B. (6–10) Complete this story. Use **he**, **she**, **it**, or **they**.

Uncle Paul listens to one song. _____ laughs out loud. "These boys have talent," Uncle Paul says. "_____ have a future." Aunt Nancy tells the family. _____ says, "_____ is a great song. These brothers are great, too. _____ need to write more songs."

18 Use a Contraction

- A **contraction** is a shorter way to say two words.

  I'm a good athlete.

  Amanda loves math. **She's** a good student.

  We're friends with many skills.

- You can join a **pronoun** and a **verb** to form a contraction. Use an apostrophe (') to take the place of the letter you leave out.

Contractions
I'm
he's, she's, it's
we're, you're, they're

1. **I am** ready to run.
   I'm ready to run.

2. **He is** the coach.
   He's the coach.

3. **They are** fast, too.
   They're fast, too.

Try It

A. **Make a contraction from the words in parentheses. Use the contraction to complete the sentence pair.**

1. This race is a big event. _____ very important. **(It is)**

2. Mom watches the race. _____ with Amanda. **(She is)**

3. Those two are alike. _____ both good listeners. **(They are)**

4. I get ready. _____ nervous about the race. **(I am)**

5. "Run fast, Kevin!" Amanda yells. "_____ a winner!" **(You are)**

B. **Complete each sentence pair. Use a contraction from the chart.**

6. Amanda is in a math contest. _____ nervous, too.

7. Mr. Ross is Amanda's teacher. _____ also the math coach.

8. The other students are ready to start. _____ very good.

9. Amanda's answer is a long one. _____ the right one!

10. Amanda and I are both winners. _____ the best!

Use Subject Pronouns

Use a **subject pronoun** in place of a noun.

Who	Use	Example	Who	Use	Example
yourself	I	**I** love all kinds of sports.	yourself and another person	we	**We** also play tennis sometimes.
someone you speak to	you	**You** swim at the city pool.	two or more people you speak to	you	**You** are very good tennis players.
one other person	he	Keaton likes football. **He** is on a team.	two or more people or things	they	Sports are great fun. **They** are good exercise, too.
	she	Sonia likes basketball. **She** plays well.			
one thing	it	Basketball is fun. **It** is Dad's favorite sport.			

Try It

A. Draw a line from each sentence to the sentence that matches it. Choose the correct pronoun.

1. **Keaton** plays football well.

2. **Football** is a rough game.

3. **Grandma** goes to every game.

4. The **fans** cheer for our team.

She cheers for Keaton.

It is fun, though.

They wave banners, too.

He plays two games each week.

B. Use the correct pronoun to complete each sentence.

   5. Basketball is a great sport. _____ is very popular, too.
   <u>It / They</u>

   6. Sonia plays on the school team. _____ works hard.
   <u>She / They</u>

   7. Mr. King is the coach. _____ is tough but fair.
   <u>He / It</u>

   8. The players listen to Mr. King. _____ want to win.
   <u>He / They</u>

   9. Sonia's ball goes to Dori. _____ goes through the hoop.
   <u>It / She</u>

   10. Sonia's parents jump up. _____ wave to Dori's parents.
   <u>She / They</u>

C. Use he, she, it, or they to answer each question.

   11. Is the pool Maria's favorite place? Yes, _____ is.

   12. Does Maria swim every afternoon? No, _____ doesn't.

   13. Do other swimmers watch Maria? Yes, _____ do.

   14. Is Maria's brother at the pool today? No, _____ isn't.

   15. Do the diving boards scare Maria? No, _____ don't.

   16. Are Maria's friends proud? Yes, _____ are.

D. Draw a line from each question to the answer that matches it. Choose the correct pronoun.

   17. Does Patrick like tennis?   Yes, they do.

   18. Does Karin play against Patrick often?   Yes, it does.

   19. Does tennis keep Patrick healthy?   No, they aren't.

   20. Is Patrick good at the game?   Yes, he does.

   21. Are the rules hard to learn?   No, she doesn't.

   22. Do some tennis players become famous?   Yes, he is.

✓ Use the Correct Pronouns

A **pronoun** is a word that refers to a **noun**. You can use a pronoun to refer to a noun in the subject of a sentence. The pronoun should match the subject of your sentence.

Yasmin loves to paint and draw.
She studies art every day.

Kimiko and Matt like to write.
They write poems.

Subject Pronouns	
Singular	**Plural**
I	we
you	you
he, she, it	they

Try It

A. **Complete each sentence. Write the correct pronoun.**

1. My friend Hannah likes to write, too. _____ has a new story.

2. The story is about her dog. _____ is a funny story.

3. David loves to sing. _____ has a good voice.

4. David has a concert tonight. _____ is nervous.

5. The concert starts at 7:00 p.m. _____ ends at 9:00 p.m.

6. Antonio and Chris are going to the concert. _____ are happy to go.

7. The people at the concert have fun. _____ enjoy the concert.

B. **(8–10) Edit the paragraph. Change the underlined <u>nouns</u> to pronouns.**

Maria likes to play piano. <u>Maria</u> takes lessons from Mr. Lim.

<u>Mr. Lim</u> is a great teacher. Maria and Mr. Lim meet every

week. <u>Maria and Mr. Lim</u> practice for one hour.

Mark Your Changes

Replace with this.

Dan plays the piano. ~~Dan~~ ^He^
plays the violin, too.

✓ Check Your Spelling
Apostrophes in Contractions

You can join some words to form contractions. A **contraction** is a short form of a word or pair of words. To write a contraction, you leave out a certain letter and use an apostrophe in its place.

Word Pair	Contraction	Example Sentence
is + not	isn't	Blaise **isn't** very tall.
are + not	aren't	Her parents **aren't** very tall either.
do + not	don't	I **don't** know why her brother is so tall.
does + not	doesn't	**Doesn't** he play basketball?
I + am	I'm	**I'm** pretty sure he does.
he + is	he's	**He's** good friends with Marci.
she + is	she's	**She's** a basketball player, too.
you + are	you're	**You're** on her team.
they + are	they're	**They're** both excellent players.

Try It

A. **Edit each sentence. Replace incorrect contractions with correct ones.**

   1. Your'e good at softball.

   2. I do'nt like to play, though.

   3. Im better at gymnastics.

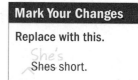

Mark Your Changes

Replace with this.

She's
~Shes short.

B. **(4–6) Read the poem. Use marks to change the underlined words to contractions.**

We <u>are not</u> just one person.

Take a look at me: <u>I am</u> a gymnast, a student, a daughter, and a friend.

I <u>do not</u> mind wearing so many hats.

What about you?

✔ Check for Sentence Punctuation

Different types of sentences use different end marks. The punctuation adds to the meaning of the sentence. It tells the reader whether the sentence is a question, a statement, or an exclamation.

- Use a **question mark** at the end of a question.
  Is Coach Fred a good coach**?**

- Use a **period** at the end of a statement or a polite command.
  He always helps us**.**

- Use an **exclamation point** to show strong feeling or surprise.
  Coach Fred is the best**!**

Try It

A. **Edit each sentence. Use the correct end mark.**

1. Does Coach Fred play soccer

2. He never gives up

3. Coach Fred plays soccer every day

4. Soccer is really fun

Mark Your Changes
Add an end mark.
Do you like soccer ⌄

B. **Change each sentence and write it on the line. Use the correct end mark.**

5. Is Coach Fred there for us? (Change to a statement.)

_____

6. He leads the way. (Change to a question.)

_____

7. Don't ever, ever give up. (Change to an exclamation.)

_____

8. Try it again! (Change to a statement.)

_____

Use the Verb *Be*

Remember: The forms of the verb **be** are **am**, **is**, and **are**. Use the form that agrees with the subject.

Singular (One)
I am from Mexico.
Are you from Mexico?
Is Ivan from Mexico? **Is he** here now?
Carmen is in my class. **She is** not here today.
Her **chair is** over there. **It is** empty.

Plural (More Than One)
My cousin and I are from Peru. **We are** not from Mexico.
Those **boys are** from Peru.
Are you girls from Peru, too?
Ten **students are** in my class. **They are** not all here today.

Try It

A. **Complete each sentence. Write the correct form of the verb.**

1. Ivan _____ my friend.
   is / are

2. I _____ happy to know him.
   am / is

3. His name _____ not hard to say.
   is / are

4. It _____ from a Spanish word for archer.
   is / are

5. _____ other names from Spanish words, too?
   Is / Are

B. **Choose a noun to complete each subject.**

6. Everyone has a name. My _____ is Lily.

7. A _____ is a kind of flower.

8. Violets are flowers, too. Is _____ a good name for a girl?

9. Rose is my friend. A _____ is another kind of flower.

10. Rose is my best friend. Best _____ are special.

REMEMBER
• A **noun** is the name of a person, place, or thing.
• A noun is often the most important word in the subject of your sentence.

Use the Verb *Do*

Remember: The forms of the verb **do** are **do** and **does**. Use the form that agrees with the subject.

Use **do** with **I**, **you**, **we**, **they**, and **plural nouns**.

Do you have photo albums?
Yes, **I** <u>do</u>.

They <u>do</u> not show some people.

My **uncles** <u>do</u> not have pictures there.

Do we want pictures? Yes, **we** <u>do</u>.

Use **does** with **he**, **she**, **it**, and **singular nouns**.

Does Eva have her camera?
Yes, **she** <u>does</u>.

Uncle Lorenzo sits quietly.
He <u>does</u> not smile.

Does his **picture** look good?
Yes, **it** <u>does</u>.

Try It

A. Complete each sentence. Write the correct form of the verb.

1. _____ you like Eva's pictures?
   Does / Do

2. _____ people look good in them?
   Does / Do

3. I _____ not see any bad pictures.
   does / do

4. _____ Eva know a lot about cameras?
   Does / Do

5. Yes, she _____ .
   does / do

B. Use the pronoun **he**, **she**, **it**, or **they** to complete each sentence pair. Underline the noun that the pronoun goes with.

6. Eva is a good friend. _____ takes good pictures, too.

7. Her ideas are fun. _____ make great pictures.

8. Sometimes her brother helps Eva. _____ tells funny jokes.

9. A camera is great. _____ is a wonderful tool.

10. Pictures show family members. _____ record the good memories.

> **REMEMBER**
>
> A **pronoun** refers to a noun.
>
> - Use **he** to talk about one boy.
> - Use **she** to talk about one girl.
> - Use **it** to talk about one thing.
> - Use **they** to talk about more than one person or thing.

Use the Verb *Have*

Remember: The forms of the verb **have** are **have** and **has**. In statements, use the form that agrees with the subject. In questions and negative statements, however, use **have** with a form of **do**.

Singular (One)
I **have** a love for stories.
Do you **have** a new story?
Does it **have** a special hero?
The hero **has** the name Pete.
He **does not have** a brother.
He **has** a sister, though.
Liz has a good time with Pete.

Plural (More Than One)
Mia and I **have** a new story.
We **have** many special stories.
Do the stories **have** strange characters?
Our **stories have** one funny character.
They **do not have** strange characters.

Try It

A. Complete each sentence. Write the correct form of the verb.

1. Pete _____ an adventure with his sister.
   has / have

2. They _____ a special bicycle for two people.
   has / have

3. It _____ two seats and two wheels.
   has / have

4. Pete _____ a plan for a bicycle trip.
   has / have

5. Do you _____ a friend like Pete?
   has / have

B. Use the pronoun I, we, or you to complete each sentence.

6. Mia and I meet later. _____ have more ideas.

7. "Do _____ have a new story?" my brother asks.

8. "Rose and _____ have the best idea!" Mia answers.

REMEMBER
• Use **I** to talk about yourself.
• Use **we** to talk about yourself and another person.
• Use **you** to talk to one or more persons.

Use Action Verbs

- An **action verb** tells what the subject does. The tense, or time, of a verb shows when an action happens. Use the present tense to tell what the subject does now or often.

   Many birds **fly** around our house.

   I **plan** a birdhouse for them.

- Add **-s** to the verb if the subject is one person or one thing (not **I** or **You**).

   Grandpa **builds** houses for people. He **gives** good advice.

Try It

A. Use a verb from the box to complete each sentence.

cuts	helps	use	work	works

1. Grandpa _____ with the birdhouse.

2. He _____ wood with a saw.

3. I _____ a hammer and nails.

4. We _____ on the birdhouse together.

5. Sometimes Mom _____ with us, too.

B. Complete each sentence. Write the correct form of the verb in parentheses.

6. Grandpa _____ a lot. **(know)**

7. I _____ from him. **(learn)**

8. Many birds _____ the birdhouse. **(visit)**

9. One bird often _____ on the roof. **(stand)**

10. Another bird _____ loud noises. **(make)**

19 Ask Questions with Action Verbs

- You can start a question with **Who** or **What**. Put the **action verb** after **Who** or **What**.

- When you answer the question, put the verb after the **subject**. You can also use **do** or **does** to answer the question.

Question	Answer
What happens first?	**Sara puts** the toy on the table.
Who helps the child?	**Sara does**.

Who plays with the toy? The child does.

Try It

A. Write the words in the correct order to ask a question. Then write an answer.

1. falls / What / from the table / ? _____

2. needs / Who / some help / ? _____

3. gives / advice / Who / ? _____

4. Who / again / tries / ? _____

B. Read the answer. Then write a question for it.

5. Sara smiles at the child. _____

6. Sara gives a block to the child. _____

7. The child places the block correctly. _____

8. The block falls off the table. _____

20 Ask Questions with Action Verbs

- You can start a question with **When** or **Where**. Use **do** or **does** with an **action verb**.

- Put **do** or **does** after **When** or **Where**. Put the subject next. Put an action verb after the subject.

- Use a statement to answer the question. Put an action verb after the subject.

Question	Answer
When does the **coach give** advice?	The **coach gives** advice before the game.
Where do the **players sit**?	The **players sit** on the bench.

Where does the coach meet with the team?

Try It

A. Write the words in the correct order to ask a question.

1. do / the players / When / practice / ? _____

2. they / practice / Where / do / ? _____

3. the coach / stand / does / Where / ? _____

4. blow / When / his whistle / the referee / does / ? _____

_____

B. Complete each question. Use **When** or **Where** and **do** or **does**.

5. _____ the players begin the game?

6. _____ the tallest player play?

7. _____ the other players run?

8. _____ the coach end the practice?

21 Make Negative Statements with Action Verbs

- To make a negative statement, put **do not** (or **don't**) or **does not** (or **doesn't**) between the **subject** and the **action verb**.

  1. Friends do not give advice.

  Friends don't give advice.

  2. Ana does not get advice.

  Ana doesn't get advice.

- Do not add **-s** to the action verb in a negative statement.

  Ana **needs** a friend.

  She does not **need** an enemy.

Try It

A. Make each statement negative. Write the negative statement.

1. Ana invites Maria to the party.

_____

2. Maria talks to Beth about the problem.

_____

3. Beth thinks for a while.

_____

4. The girls discuss solutions.

_____

B. Write the words in the correct order to make negative statements.

5. suggest / Beth / good ideas / does not / . _____

6. Maria / Beth's ideas / help / do not / . _____

7. does not / a solution / Maria / have / . _____

8. offer / does not / Beth / other ideas / . _____

22 Use the Right Form of the Action Verb

Add **-s** to an **action verb** to tell about one person, place, or thing (not **I** or **You**).

Carlos **work<u>s</u>** after school.

He **help<u>s</u>** at his father's store.

Mr. Suarez **sell<u>s</u>** groceries.

Carlos helps his father.

Try It

A. Underline the verb in each sentence. Then use the verb in another sentence.

1. Carlos stacks the fruit.

_____

2. Mr. Suarez gives advice to Carlos.

_____

3. A customer comes into the store.

_____

4. The customer buys some vegetables.

_____

B. Write a verb to complete each sentence. Make sure the verb goes with the subject.

5. Carlos _____ a lot about the store.

6. He _____ about new ideas for the store.

7. Carlos _____ his ideas to his father.

8. Mr. Suarez _____ good advice from Carlos!

23 Use the Right Form of the Action Verb

- **Action verbs** change to go with the **subject** of a sentence.

- Add **-s** to the verb if the subject is **he, she, it,** or a singular noun (not **I** or **You**).

    Some **students study** music.

    They practice every day.

    Tina plays the flute.

    She learns a lot from her music teacher.

The girls play their instruments.

Try It

A. Use words from the columns to write sentences. Make sure the verbs go with the subjects.

Subject	Verb	Rest of Sentence
Rachel	gives	their music together.
The girls	joins	advice about the flute to Tina.
Jon	practice	Tina's class.

1. _____

2. _____

3. _____

B. Write a verb to complete each sentence. Make sure the verb goes with the subject.

4. The students _____ in the band concert.

5. Tina's mom _____ to the music.

6. She _____ after the concert.

24 Use *Needs to*, *Wants to*, and *Has to*

- Sometimes you use **to** and an **action verb** after **needs**, **wants**, and **has**.

  Luisa **needs to get** a summer job.

  Her teacher **wants to help** her.

- Use the right form of the first verb to go with the **subject**. Do not add **-s** to the verb that follows **to**.

  I have to find a job, too.

  Our **parents want to give** us advice.

Try It

A. Use words from the columns to write sentences. Make sure the verbs go with the subjects.

Subject	Verb	Rest of Sentence
Luisa	has	to hire her for the summer.
Two stores	needs	to make a wise choice.
She	want	to choose one job.

1. _____

2. _____

3. _____

B. Complete each sentence. Write the correct form of **needs to**, **wants to**, or **has to**, followed by an **action verb**.

4. Luisa _____ at the clothing store.

5. She _____ her parents first.

6. They _____ that she can work there.

Use Action Verbs in the Present Tense

PAST	PRESENT	FUTURE
(before now)	(now)	(after now)

- Use the **present tense** of a verb to talk about something that happens now or often.

    My friends **make** wise decisions.

    We **listen** to advice. Sometimes we **give** good advice.

- Add **-s** to the verb if the subject is one person or one thing (not **I** or **You**).

    Maria **needs** advice. Helga **gives** advice to Maria.

- To form a question, put **Do** or **Does** before the subject.

    Do friends give good advice to James?

    Does James listen to their advice?

- To form a negative statement, put **do not** (or **don't**) or **does not** (or **doesn't**) between the subject and the verb.

    James **doesn't** ask for advice.

    His friends **do not** give him advice.

Try It

A. Complete each sentence. Write the correct verb.

1. Wise people _____ from other people.
   learn / learns

2. Maria _____ Helga for advice.
   ask / asks

3. Helga _____ Maria.
   help / helps

4. Now Maria's friends _____ advice from Helga.
   want / wants

5. They _____ about Helga's wisdom.
   know / knows

6. Helga _____ an advice column for the school newspaper.
   plan / plans

B. Complete each sentence. Write the correct form of the verb.

   7. Helga _____ with the guidance counselor. **(talk)**

   8. The guidance counselor _____ to help. **(want)**

   9. They _____ permission from the principal. **(get)**

  10. Helga's friends _____ on a name for the column. **(vote)**

  11. They _____ the name "Words of Wisdom." **(choose)**

  12. The advice column _____ on Monday. **(begin)**

  13. The first writer _____ about meeting new friends. **(ask)**

  14. Helga _____ her first "Words of Wisdom." **(write)**

C. Write each statement as a question. Use Do or Does.

  15. Helga has advice for me. _____

  16. The advice column gives good advice. _____

  17. Many students ask for advice. _____

  18. They write about their problems. _____

  19. A wise person listens to Helga's advice. _____

  _____

  20. Helga acts in a wise way. _____

D. Write each statement as a negative statement.

  21. I need advice. _____

  22. The advice helps me. _____

  23. My friends write advice for the advice column. _____

  _____

  24. Helga works on the column alone. _____

  _____

Use Present Progressive Verbs

PAST   PRESENT   FUTURE

(before now)   (now)   (after now)

- Sometimes you want to talk about something that you do often. Use the **present tense**.

    I **visit** Grandma and Grandpa every Saturday.

- At other times you want to talk about what you are doing now. Use the **present progressive** form of the verb.

    I **am talking** with Grandpa now.

I am visiting Grandpa.

- To form a **present progressive** verb, use **am**, **is**, or **are** plus the **-ing** form of the action verb.

    I **am learning** from Grandpa.

    He **is telling** me about his life.

    We **are talking** about his childhood.

Try It

A. Complete each sentence. Write the present progressive form of the verb in parentheses.

1. Grandpa _____ to me. **(speak)**

2. We _____ family relationships. **(discuss)**

3. I _____ carefully. **(listen)**

B. Add a verb to complete each sentence. Use the present progressive form.

4. My grandparents _____ me today.

5. Grandma _____ me pictures of Grandpa.

6. He _____ football in them.

25 Use a Helping Verb

- Sometimes you can use the **present progressive** form of a verb to talk about what you are doing now.

- To form a present progressive verb, use a **helping verb** with an **action verb**.

- **Am**, **is**, and **are** can be helping verbs. Use **am**, **is**, or **are** with the **-ing** form of the action verb. The helping verb must agree with the subject.

  I **am reading** a magazine article.

  The writer **is telling** about teens.

  The teens **are following** good advice.

Try It

A. Complete each sentence. Write the correct verb.

1. This magazine _____ me how to make good decisions.
   is teaching / are teaching

2. The writer _____ several experts.
   am interviewing / is interviewing

3. She _____ good questions.
   is asking / are asking

4. They _____ about school bullies.
   is talking / are talking

B. Complete each sentence. Write am, is, or are and the -ing form of the verb in parentheses.

5. I _____ with a bully at school. **(deal)**

6. The experts _____ good advice. **(offer)**

7. They _____ me what to do. **(tell)**

8. I _____ from them. **(learn)**

26 Ask a Question

- You can use the **present progressive** to ask a question about something that is happening now.
- Start the question with **Am**, **Is**, or **Are**. Put the **subject** between the **helping verb** and the **action verb**. Make sure the helping verb agrees with the subject.
- Answer with a statement. Put the subject before the helping verb.

Question	Answer
Am I reading a book?	Yes, **I am**.
Is Tyrell looking at pictures?	Yes, **he is**.
Are they showing famous paintings?	Yes, **they are**.

Try It

A. Write the words in the correct order to ask a question.

1. Tyrell / Is / reading / about a famous painter / ? _____

_____

2. learning / about art / he / Is / ? _____

3. the pictures / filling / the whole page / Are / ? _____

_____

4. they / teaching / Are / Tyrell / how to paint / ? _____

_____

B. Complete each question. Use **am**, **is**, or **are** and an action verb that ends in **-ing**.

5. _____ I _____ about art?

6. _____ my art teachers _____ me?

27 Make a Negative Statement

- You can use a negative statement to tell what is **not** happening now.
- Use **am**, **is**, or **are** with an **action verb** that ends in **-ing**.
- Put **not** between the **helping verb** and the action verb.
  Ms. Reyes **is teaching** Dan.
  She **is not singing** with him.
  They **are playing** music.
  They **are not playing** basketball.

Ms. Reyes is not playing the piano.

Try It

A. **Make each statement negative. Write what is not happening now.**

1. Other students are playing drums.

_____

2. The piano player is helping Ms. Reyes.

_____

3. I am reading a book about music.

_____

4. Ms. Reyes is teaching Dan to play the trumpet.

_____

B. **Write negative statements. Put the words in the correct order.**

5. is / Ms. Reyes / singing / not / a song / . _____

6. giving / are / advice / The students / to Ms. Reyes / not / . _____

_____

7. We / not / performing / on a stage / are / . _____

8. not / playing / am / I / my music / . _____

28 Use Helping Verbs: *Can* and *May*

- A verb can have two parts: a **helping verb** and a **main verb**. The main verb shows the action. Sometimes a helping verb changes the meaning of the main verb.

- Use the helping verb **can** to tell about what someone is able to do.

    Emilio **can ask** for advice from his parents.

- Use the helping verb **may** to say that something is possible.

    He **may talk** to them after school today.

- **Can** and **may** stay the same with all subjects. Do not add **-s**.

Try It

A. Write **can** or **may** to complete each sentence. Use the clue in parentheses.

1. Emilio _____ study a world language next year. **(possible)**

2. He _____ take either French or Chinese. **(able)**

3. He _____ study music instead. **(possible)**

4. Emilio's parents _____ help him. **(able)**

5. They _____ have some good ideas. **(possible)**

6. Sometimes parents _____ give good advice! **(able)**

B. Write **can** or **may** and a main verb to complete each sentence.

7. Emilio's friend _____ Chinese in school.

8. She _____ a little Chinese already.

9. Emilio _____ Chinese, too.

10. Then they _____ together!

29 Use Helping Verbs: *Must* and *Should*

- A verb can have two parts: a **helping verb** and a **main verb**. The main verb shows the action. Sometimes the helping verb changes the meaning of the main verb.

- Use the helping verb **must** to tell about something that is very important to do.

    Isabel **must find** a part-time job.

- Use the helping verb **should** to give advice or show what you believe.

    She **should get** advice from her guidance counselor.

- **Must** and **should** stay the same with all subjects. Do not add **-s**.

Try It

A. Write **must** or **should** to complete each sentence. Use the clue in parentheses.

1. Isabel _____ look in the newspaper. **(advice)**

2. She _____ read the ads. **(important)**

3. Isabel _____ apply for many jobs. **(advice)**

4. She _____ dress nicely. **(advice)**

5. She _____ choose the best job! **(important)**

B. Write **must** or **should** and a main verb to complete each sentence.

6. The store manager _____ good advice to Isabel.

7. Isabel _____ quickly.

8. She _____ her job.

30 Ask Questions with Helping Verbs

- You can start a question with **Can**, **May**, or **Should**. Put the **subject** between the **helping verb** and the **main verb**
- When you answer the question, put the subject before the helping verb.
- If the answer is negative, put **not** between the helping verb and the main verb.

Question	Answer
May I ask for advice?	Yes, **you may ask** for advice. No, **you may not ask** for advice.
Should I join the drama club?	Yes, **you should join** the club. No, **you should not join** the club.

Can you talk right now? Yes, I can.

Try It

A. Write the words in the correct order to ask a question. Then write the answer to the question.

1. ask / Luisa / June / for her opinion / May / ? _____

    _____

2. give / Can / to Luisa / June / advice / ? _____

    _____

3. another club / Luisa / Should / try / ? _____

    _____

B. Write a question for each answer. Then write a negative answer to the question.

4. Luisa should join the debate team. _____

    _____

5. June can tell Luisa what to do. _____

    _____

Use Helping Verbs

Sometimes you use two verbs that work together: a **helping verb** and a **main verb**. The main verb shows the action.

My grandmother **can sew**.

Sometimes a helping verb changes the meaning of the main verb.

- Use **can** to tell about what someone is able to do.

    My grandmother **can make** her own clothes.

- Use **may** to tell about something that is possible.

    She **may teach** me.

- Use **should** to give advice or show what you believe.

    I **should learn** from her.

- Use **must** to tell about something that is very important to do.

    I **must** ask her for sewing lessons.

Can, **may**, **should**, and **must** stay the same with all subjects. Do not add **-s**.

Grandma **can design** quilts.

She **should start** a quilt-making class.

Try It

A. Write a helping verb from the box to complete each sentence. More than one answer is possible.

can	may	must	should

1. Grandma _____ make a quilt about her life.

2. She _____ show a different picture in each square.

3. I _____ share my idea with Grandma.

4. She _____ agree with me.

5. Then we _____ work on the quilt together.

B. Write a helping verb for each sentence. Use the clue in parentheses.

6. Grandma _____ go to the store. **(able to)**

7. She _____ take me along. **(possible)**

8. We _____ get material for the quilt. **(important)**

9. Some of the material _____ have flowers. **(believe)**

10. Grandma _____ cut out all the squares. **(important)**

11. I _____ help her. **(believe)**

12. She _____ teach her skills to me. **(able to)**

13. I _____ be ready to learn them all! **(possible)**

C. Add **can, may, should,** or **must** to complete each sentence.

14. We _____ work on the quilt every day.

15. I _____ find time after school.

16. The quilt _____ take about three months to make.

17. It _____ take a little longer, though.

18. We _____ finish before my birthday.

19. Grandma _____ share her wisdom with me.

20. Then I _____ sew as well as Grandma.

D. Add **can, may, should,** or **must** and a main verb. More than one answer is possible.

21. Grandma _____ now.

22. She _____ proud.

23. She _____ the most beautiful quilts ever.

24. I _____ her quilts to my friends.

Use Nouns and Verbs in Sentences

- A noun names a person, an animal, a place, or a thing. A noun can be the **subject** of a sentence.

    The **firefighters** work hard.
         subject

- A noun can also be part of the predicate when it relates to the verb. We call it an **object**.

    The firefighters take **classes**.
        verb   object

- Many English sentences follow the Subject-Verb-Object, or SVO, pattern.

    Firefighters use **equipment**.
      subject   verb   object

    Equipment protects the **firefighters**.
      subject   verb   object

Firefighters perform dangerous tasks.

Try It

A. Read each sentence. Is the underlined noun a subject or an object? Write **subject** or **object** on the line.

  1. <u>Instructors</u> are teaching the firefighters. _____

  2. Some <u>students</u> are practicing rescues. _____

  3. One firefighter is using a <u>rope</u>. _____

B. Write a word from the box to complete each sentence.

Subject	Verb	Object
helpers	fight	houses

  4. Some fires burn _____ .

  5. Firefighters _____ the fires.

  6. These brave _____ save many lives.

31 Use Subject Nouns

- A **noun** names a person, an animal, a place, or a thing. A noun is the most important word in the **subject** of a sentence.

- The word **the** often comes before a **subject noun**.

  The **cookbook** belongs to Joseph's father.

  The **father** is a chef.

  His **restaurant** is downtown.

Subject Nouns	
person	father
place	restaurant
thing	cookbook

Try It

A. Complete each sentence. Write a noun from the box.

chef	dinner	kitchen	sink	son

1. _____ is rice and beans today.

2. The _____ teaches his son.

3. The _____ needs to pay attention.

4. The _____ is full of dishes.

5. The _____ is a mess now.

B. Write a noun to complete each sentence.

6. The _____ is a place to learn about food.

7. The _____ is in the refrigerator.

8. The _____ cleans up the kitchen.

(32) Use Plural Nouns

- A **plural noun** names more than one person, place, or thing.

  Many **animals** live in the wild.

- Add **-s** to most nouns to make them plural.

  Animals in the wild are smart.

  Ants are hard **workers**.

- Some nouns end in **s**, **z**, **sh**, **ch**, or **x**. Add **-es** to those nouns to make them plural.

  Some ants climb on the **branches** of trees.

- In a sentence, be sure the **verb** agrees with a **plural subject noun**. Do not add **-s** to the verb.

  The **ants eat** leaves there.

The ants carry leaves.

Try It

A. Complete each sentence. Write the correct noun.

1. The _____ run in the snow.
   fox / foxes

2. A _____ eats small animals for lunch.
   fox / foxes

3. Foxes eat many _____, too.
   grasshopper / grasshoppers

4. This _____ blends in with the plants in a field.
   insect / insects

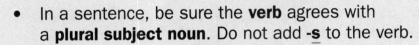

B. Add the noun in parentheses to each sentence. Add **-s** or **-es** to make the noun plural.

5. _____ in the wild are wise. **(animal)**

6. Some _____ blend in with plants in the forest. **(insect)**

7. _____ are homes for some birds. **(bush)**

8. Birds also hide in the leafy _____ of trees. **(branch)**

33 Use Subject Nouns and Pronouns

- A pronoun refers to a **noun** in a sentence. If the noun is part of the subject, use a **subject pronoun**. **He**, **she**, **it**, and **they** are some subject pronouns.

- The subject pronoun must go with the noun it refers to.

- Use **he** to talk about a boy or a man. Use **she** to talk about a girl or a woman.

  Julia loves music. **She** listens to music all the time.

  Her **brother** loves music, too. **He** downloads songs on his computer.

  The **computer** is full of music. **It** has hundreds of songs.

  Julia's **parents** love music. **They** share this love with their children.

Try It

A. Underline the noun in the first sentence that goes with the <u>pronoun</u> in the second sentence. Use the pronoun in a new sentence.

1. This store sells music. <u>It</u> has many kinds of music.

_____

2. Julia and Kris look at music. <u>They</u> want to buy some.

_____

3. Julia buys these songs. <u>She</u> sings songs with her family.

_____

B. Write a pronoun to finish the second sentence in each pair.

4. Composers are creative people. _____ write music.

5. Julia writes music, too. _____ plays her songs on a guitar.

34 Use Subject and Object Pronouns

- Use a **subject pronoun** as the **subject** of a sentence.

  Marta needs a new dress. **She** is at the mall.
  subject   subject

  The **mall** is big. **It** has too many clothes!
  subject   subject

- Use an **object pronoun** as the **object** of the verb.

  Clara sees **Marta**. Clara helps **her**.
  verb   object   verb object

  Clara finds a pretty **dress**. Marta takes **it** to the mirror.
  verb   object   verb object

- Notice that the pronouns **you** and **it** are the same in both subject and object forms.

Pronouns	
Subject	**Object**
I	me
you	you
he	him
she	her
it	it

Try It

A. Write the correct pronoun to finish each pair of sentences. Underline the noun it stands for.

1. Clara chooses the dress. Marta likes _____ , too.
   it / him

2. Marta buys the dress. _____ leaves the store.
   She / Her

3. Marta thanks Clara. Then Marta takes _____ to the ice cream store.
   her / him

4. They see Marco there. They ask _____ for ice cream.
   he / him

B. (5–8) Complete the paragraph. Write the correct subject or object pronouns from the chart.

Clara needs a book. _____ asks Marta for advice. Marta chooses a

book. _____ is Marta's favorite. Marta shows _____ to Clara.

Clara takes the book to the salesman. _____ sells the book to Clara.

35 Name Yourself Last

Subject Pronoun: I

- Use the pronoun **I** in the **subject** of a sentence.

    I am a student at Elm Street High School.

- Sometimes you talk about somebody else and yourself. Use the pronoun **I** last.

    Michael and I arrive at school.

    He and I see a new student.

Object Pronoun: me

- Use the pronoun **me** as the **object**. The new student approaches **me**.

- Sometimes you talk about somebody else and yourself. Use the pronoun **me** last.

    Mia meets **Michael and me**.

    She asks **him and me** for help.

Try It

A. Write **I** or **me** to complete each sentence.

1. Mia and _____ go to the guidance office.

2. The guidance counselor and _____ tell Mia about the school.

3. Mia asks my friends and _____ for directions to the cafeteria.

4. Mia and _____ are friends by the end of the day.

5. She thanks Michael and _____ for our help.

B. Write a noun and **I** or **me** to complete each sentence.

6. Mia invites _____ to her house.

7. _____ both go.

8. Mia greets _____ at the front door.

9. _____ play video games with Mia.

10. _____ make plans to hang out on Saturday.

36 Use Subject and Object Pronouns

- Use a **subject pronoun** as the **subject** of a sentence. To talk about more than one, use **we**, **you**, or **they**.

  Friends help each other. **They** give advice.

subject   subject

- Use an **object pronoun** as the **object** of the verb. To talk about more than one, use **us**, **you**, or **them**.

  Benita has many **friends**. She helps **them**.

object   object

  We are Benita's friends. Benita helps **us**.

subject   object

Pronouns	
Subject	**Object**
we	us
you	you
they	them

Try It

A. Write the correct pronoun to complete each pair of sentences.

1. We help our friends. Our friends help _____ , too.

we / us

2. My friend Benita has two dogs. Sometimes I walk _____ for Benita.

they / them

3. The dogs are Great Danes. _____ are huge dogs.

They / Them

4. Sometimes Benita bathes the dogs. I spray _____ with water from the hose.

they / them

5. The dogs lick us. _____ pet them.

We / Us

B. (6–10) Complete the paragraph. Write the correct pronouns from the chart.

We have a shoe store. Sometimes _____ need help. Benita

helps _____ . My parents order boxes of shoes. Benita unpacks

_____ . My parents like Benita. _____ teach her about

the business. Benita likes my parents, too. They are wise. Benita respects

_____ .

Use Object Pronouns

- Remember that a **noun** can be the object of a verb.

    I respect the **animals**. I protect the **animals**.
       verb   object   verb   object

- A pronoun refers to a noun in a sentence. If the noun is the object of a verb, special forms of pronouns are used. These are called **object pronouns**.

    I respect the **animals**. I protect **them**.
       verb   object   verb   object
                                              pronoun

- Study the subject and object pronouns. An object pronoun is always the object of a verb.

Subject Pronoun	I	you	he	she	it	we	they
Object Pronoun	me	you	him	her	it	us	them

- Notice that the pronouns **you** and **it** are the same in both subject and object forms.

Try It

A. Complete the second sentence in each pair. Write the object pronoun that refers to the underlined words.

1. Respect <u>the Earth</u>. Keep _____ clean.

2. Do not throw <u>papers</u> on the ground. Recycle _____.

3. Let <u>animals</u> live in their homes. Do not hurt _____.

4. Watch <u>the mother deer</u>. Can you photograph _____?

5. Walk <u>your dog</u> in the woods. Keep _____ on a leash.

6. <u>I</u> protect the Earth. Help _____.

B. **Write the correct pronoun to complete each sentence.**

7. Our teacher takes _____ on a hike in the woods.
   <u>we / us</u>

8. _____ points out the plants.
   <u>He / Him</u>

9. The students study _____.
   <u>they / them</u>

10. Sara looks around. _____ collects some leaves.
    <u>She / Her</u>

11. Sara puts _____ in a collection bag.
    <u>they / them</u>

12. _____ can look at the leaves under the microscope at school.
    <u>We / Us</u>

C. **(13–22) Write pronouns to complete the sentences.**

Mr. Chin takes my classmates and me to a pond. _____ shows

_____ many interesting things there. First _____ see a

frog. _____ sits on a lily pad.

Robert sees some fish in the water. _____ watches

_____. Sara asks _____ about the fish. "_____

think those fish are tadpoles," Robert tells _____. "_____

become frogs."

D. **Write a pronoun to complete the answer to each question.**

23. Who takes my classmates and me on a hike? Mr. Chin takes _____.

24. Where do you see some frogs? I see _____ in the pond.

25. Where does Sara use a microscope? _____ uses a microscope at school.

26. What does Robert tell Sara? _____ tells _____ about tadpoles.

✓ # Check for Subject-Verb Agreement

Remember that the **subject** and **verb** in a sentence must agree in number.

- Add **-s** to an action verb if the subject is **he**, **she**, **it**, or a **singular noun**. Do not add anything if the subject is **I**, **you**, **we**, **they**, or a **plural noun**.

  Tamika gives advice to her friends.
  They listen to her.

- Use the correct form of the verbs **be**, **do**, and **have**.

I	am	do	have
he, she, it, singular noun	is	does	has
you, we, they, plural noun	are	do	have

Try It

A. Complete each sentence. Write the correct form of the verb in parentheses.

1. Nick _____ a problem. **(have)**

2. He _____ to go to Celia's party, but he also _____ to study. **(want, need)**

3. Tamika _____ him to study first and go to the party afterward. **(tell)**

4. Nick's friends _____ with Tamika. **(agree)**

5. She _____ so wise. **(be)**

B. (6–10) Edit the paragraph. Fix the verbs that do not agree with their subject.

   Casi am worried. She have two tests on Friday. A study group is meeting on Thursday night, but Casi work every Thursday until 9:00 p.m. She talk to her coworker Amanda. Amanda needs to earn more money. She wants to work for Casi on Thursday. Casi's problem is solved. Both girls is happy.

Mark Your Changes

Replace with this.

Amanda ~~need~~ a job.
     needs

✓ Check Your Spelling

Plural Nouns

Use these rules for forming plural nouns:

Rules	Examples
Make most nouns plural by adding **-s** to the end.	**problem ⟶ problems** **test ⟶ tests**
If the noun ends in **s**, **sh**, **ch**, **x**, or **z**, add **-es**.	**wish ⟶ wishes** **box ⟶ boxes**
If the noun ends in **y**, change the **y** to **i** and add **-es**.	**lady ⟶ ladies** **penny ⟶ pennies**

Try It

A. **Complete each sentence. Write the plural of the noun in parentheses.**

1. I'm so angry with my younger _____. **(brother)**

2. They always act like _____ and don't help with anything. **(baby)**

3. For example, I have to wash all the _____ after dinner by myself. **(dish)**

4. How can I get them to help with household _____? **(duty)**

B. **(5–8) Edit the advice column. Find and fix four spelling errors.**

Dear Angry,

It can seem unfair when the younger kides don't work as hard as you do. Try to get your brothers to help you. Maybe they can wash plates and you can wash glasss. Make the chores seem fun. You can give your brothers rewardes for helping you. Would they like boxs of baseball cards?

—Problem-Solver

Mark Your Changes

Replace with this.

         parents
Tell your ~~parentes~~ how you feel.

✔ Check for Capital Letters

Always capitalize the names of people and their titles. Also, remember to capitalize the pronoun **I**.

Rules	Examples
Capitalize proper nouns.	**A**bigail **V**an **B**uren **D**r. **J**oyce **B**rothers
Capitalize the pronoun **I** every time it appears in a sentence.	**I** am writing to you because **I** need some advice.
Do not capitalize common nouns.	The **c**olumnist answered my letter.

Try It

A. Edit each sentence. Correct capitalization errors.

   1. I ask mr. Phillips for some advice.

   2. He is my favorite Teacher.

   3. He gives me some excellent Ideas.

   4. Now i know how to solve my problem.

Mark Your Changes

Capitalize.

  i̲ have a problem.

Make lowercase.

  Tell your ℓounselor.

B. Complete each sentence. Remember to capitalize correctly.

   5. I give advice to _____.

   6. The problem is _____.

   7. One good solution is _____.

   8. Another solution is _____.

Use Action Verbs

Remember: An **action verb** tells what the subject does. Use the **present tense** to tell what the subject does now or often.

- **Action verbs** change to go with the subject. Add **-s** to the verb if the subject is one person or one thing (not **I** or **you**).

  I always **learn** from my teacher.

  My teacher **learns** from me, too.

- To form a question, put **do** or **does** before the subject.

  What **do** you learn at school?

  Does your teacher help you?

- To form a negative statement, put **do not (don't)** or **does not (doesn't)** between the subject and the verb. Do not add **-s** to the verb.

  We **do not (don't)** go to school on Saturday.

  Dad **does not (doesn't)** work on Saturday, either.

Try It

A. Complete each sentence. Write the correct form of the verb.

1. Wise adults _____ their wisdom.
   share / shares

2. My doctor _____ me advice.
   give / gives

3. She _____ not want me to overeat.
   do / does

4. I always _____ healthy snacks.
   eat / eats

B. Complete each sentence. Write the correct form of the verb in parentheses.

5. My science teacher _____ me, too. **(help)**

6. She _____ me about food choices. **(tell)**

7. Now I _____ more about my health. **(know)**

8. _____ a wise adult help you stay healthy? **(do)**

Use Helping Verbs

Remember: A verb can have two parts: a **helping verb** and a **main verb**. The main verb shows the action.

- Use the **present progressive** form of a verb to talk about what you are doing now. To form a present progressive verb, use a **helping verb** with an **action verb**.

- **Am**, **is**, and **are** can be helping verbs. Use **am**, **is**, or **are** plus the **-ing** form of the action verb to form the present progressive.

   I **am visiting** Great-Aunt Rose.

   She **is talking** to Mom and Dad.

   We **are spending** her birthday together.

Try It

A. Complete each sentence. Write the present progressive form of the verb in parentheses.

1. I _____ about plants in school. **(study)**

2. Great-Aunt Rose _____ me. **(help)**

3. We _____ in her garden. **(walk)**

4. She _____ me about each plant. **(tell)**

5. I _____ many things from her. **(learn)**

B. Write can or may and a main verb to complete each sentence.

6. Great-Aunt Rose _____ slowly sometimes.

7. _____ she _____ many things with me?

8. Yes, she can. We _____ to the movies together.

9. In fact, I _____ her to a movie today.

10. I _____ a lot from Great-Aunt Rose.

> **REMEMBER**
>
> Some helping verbs change the meaning of the main verb.
>
> - Use **can** to tell about what someone is able to do.
>
> - Use **may** to tell about something that is possible.

Use Singular and Plural Nouns

Remember: A **noun** can be singular or plural. It can be the subject or the object of a sentence. The verb must agree with the subject noun.

- English sentences often follow the Subject-Verb-Object, or SVO, pattern. A **noun** can be the subject or object of the sentence.

    People need **wisdom**.
    subject   verb   object

- Add **-s** to most nouns to make them plural.

    Newspapers have many good **ideas**.

- Add **-es** to nouns that end in **s**, **z**, **sh**, **ch**, or **x**.

    Coaches share advice. People also take **classes**.

Try It

A. Write a noun from the box to complete each sentence. Make the noun plural if necessary.

Subject	Object
brother	class
computer	recipe
student	

1. The _____ is a good source of information.

2. My two _____ read the news online.

3. Mom finds many _____ online, too.

4. People take _____ to learn computer skills.

5. The _____ in my class use the computer a lot.

B. Complete each sentence. Use the correct form of the noun.

6. Today, I am researching _____ at the library.
    foxs / foxes

7. I use different _____ .
    book / books

8. The librarian gives _____ for research.
    tip / tips

9. Her wisdom helps _____ .
    studentes / students

10. She understands our many _____ .
    stress / stresses

Use Adjectives Before Nouns

- **Adjectives** are words that describe people, places, or things. You can use **adjectives** to describe how something looks.

    Our **silver** plane lands in Chicago.

- An **adjective** often comes before the **noun** it describes.

    I take my **small backpack** from under the **flat seat**.

- **Adjectives** help the reader imagine what you are writing about.

    My dad rolls his suitcase down the **long** ramp.

Try It

A. Complete each sentence. Write an adjective from the box.

square	**tall**	**white**

Some buildings have **flat roofs**.

1. I like to look up at the _____ buildings.

2. They seem to touch the _____ clouds!

3. That building has _____ windows.

B. Complete each sentence. Write an adjective and a noun from the box.

Adjectives	Nouns
big **wide**	**baby** **sidewalk**
tiny	**bag**

4. We walk along the _____.

5. One man is carrying a _____ of groceries.

6. A woman pushes her _____ in a stroller.

37 Use Adjectives Before Nouns

- Some **adjectives** describe by telling how many. They come before the person, place, or thing they are describing.

  Rena plays a game at the park with her **three** cousins.

  One tree is very wide. Rena hides behind it.

- You can use adjectives like **some** or **many** when you are not sure of the exact number of something.

  The park has **many** trees.

  Some trees are very tall.

Try It

A. Complete each sentence. Write an adjective from the box.

one	two	four	many

1. I talk to _____ families at the park.

2. Rena's family sits together at _____ table.

3. Her brother sees _____ friends from school.

4. Rena plays near a pond with _____ ducks.

B. Complete each sentence. Write an adjective that tells how many.

5. _____ families at the park fly kites.

6. That kite has _____ stripes on it.

7. _____ children in Rena's family play baseball.

8. Angel hits _____ home runs!

38 Use Adjectives Before Nouns

Adjectives can describe by telling how something sounds, feels, or tastes.

Sid's home is in a **cold** climate.
Loud winds howl outside.

Rosa lives in the **hot** desert.
Quiet breezes blow at night.

Try It

A. Complete each sentence. Write an adjective from the box.

noisy	sharp	smooth	warm

1. Sid ice-skates on the _____ ice.

2. His ice skates have _____ blades.

3. He hears the _____ shouts of children.

4. Aunt Ella gives Sid a _____ cup of cocoa.

B. Complete each sentence. Write an adjective that describes how something sounds, feels, or tastes.

5. Rosa walks across the _____ desert sand.

6. She touches the _____ needles of one cactus.

7. She hears the _____ song of a bird.

8. The _____ wind blows across the sand.

39 Use Adjectives After *Am, Is,* and *Are*

- Most of the time, an **adjective** comes before the **noun** it describes.

  My class likes the **new museum**. We see **tall statues**.

- If a sentence has the verb **am, is,** or **are,** you can put the adjective after the **verb**.

  The museum **is new**. The statues **are tall**.

  My friends **are happy** to be here. Pedro **is curious** about art.

Try It

A. Complete each sentence. Choose an adjective from the box.

curious	happy	peaceful	scary	upset

1. I am _____ to see the beautiful colors.

2. Some paintings have interesting shapes in them. Kim is _____ about them.

3. Some paintings make me feel calm. They are _____.

4. Other paintings make me feel afraid. They are _____.

5. Sophia does not like the painting about war. She is _____.

B. Write an adjective to complete each sentence.

6. Taro is _____ about the artists.

7. He is _____ to be an artist.

8. We ask good questions. Our teacher is _____.

9. Devon wants to eat lunch. He is _____.

10. I want to see more art. I am _____ to go.

40 Use Demonstrative Adjectives: *This* and *That*

A **demonstrative adjective** tells if something is near or far.

- Use **this** to tell about something near to you.

I like **this** dress.

- Use **that** to tell about something far from you.

I want to buy **that** shoe over there.

Try It

A. Complete each sentence. Use the correct adjective.

1. I like _____ hat in my hand.

this / that

2. Do you like _____ shirt on the far wall?

this / that

3. Is _____ sweater over there on sale?

this / that

4. _____ shirt in front of me is bright.

This / That

5. _____ scarf on the top shelf is my favorite!

This / That

B. Complete each sentence. Write **this** or **that**.

6. We are here at the new mall. I like _____ mall a lot.

7. Dad wants to get a shirt at _____ store over there.

8. I hold up a blue shirt. "Do you like _____ shirt?" I ask.

9. Mom likes _____ yellow shirt over there on the top shelf.

10. Dad chooses a shirt. "I like _____ shirt the best!"

41 Use Demonstrative Adjectives: *These* and *Those*

A **demonstrative adjective** tells if something is near or far.

- Use **these** to tell about things that are near you.

These drawings here are my artwork.

- Use **those** to tell about things that are far from you.

My older brother made **those** paintings over there.

Try It

A. Complete each sentence. Use the correct adjective.

1. I like _____ paintings over there.
   these / those

2. I will buy _____ mugs in front of me.
   these / those

3. _____ earrings in my hand are beautiful!
   These / Those

4. Kiku painted _____ vases on the top shelf.
   these / those

5. I like _____ pots over by the door.
   these / those

B. Complete each sentence. Write **these** or **those**.

6. I point to baskets on the far wall. "I like _____ baskets," I say.

7. Dara touches some beads. "_____ beads match my skirt," she tells me.

8. "Let's look at _____ tables over there," I say.

9. I pick up some plates. "I like _____ dishes."

10. "Did you see _____ mugs on the far shelf?" Dara asks.

42 Use Demonstrative Adjectives

A **demonstrative adjective** tells if things are near or far.

Near	Far
This soup is very hot.	May I have **that** sandwich over there?
These vegetables here look fresh.	I would like **those** cookies on the top shelf.

Demonstrative Adjectives	
Singular	**Plural**
this	these
that	those

Try It

A. Choose **this, that, these,** or **those** to complete each sentence.

1. I want _____ can of soda on the top shelf.
   this / that

2. _____ cupcakes over there are from a bakery.
   That / Those

3. _____ ice cream sandwich right here looks tasty.
   This / These

4. I like _____ muffins in my hands.
   these / those

5. _____ yogurt bar on the poster over there looks real.
   This / That

B. Complete each sentence. Write **this, that, these,** or **those**.

6. Julio stares at the case. "Do _____ sandwiches in back look good?" he asks.

7. He points. "I'll take _____ one, Ms. Chen."

8. I look at my own tray. "I think _____ soup will taste delicious!"

9. "I don't know if I can eat all _____ carrots right here," I tell Julio.

10. Julio holds up his sandwich. "_____ is a great lunch," he says.

Use Adjectives

- **Adjectives** describe people, places, or things. Use adjectives to describe how something looks, sounds, feels, tastes, or smells.

   We make a **delicious** meal.

- Use adjectives to tell how many.

   Six people help.

- Most of the time, adjectives come before **nouns**.

   Luis washes **green peppers**. Eva chops **sweet onions**.

- Sometimes adjectives come after **am**, **is**, or **are**.

   The cooks **are busy** in the kitchen. We **are hungry**!

Try It

A. Complete each sentence. Choose an adjective from the box.

blue	fresh	juicy	large	little	many	sweet	two

1. My whole family makes food together. We have _____ cooks.

2. Mom bakes _____ bread. It smells delicious!

3. She takes a _____ piece for herself. She doesn't eat much.

4. Carlos squeezes _____ lemons to make lemonade.

5. Luisa adds sugar. She likes _____ lemonade.

6. The twins want their own cakes. I bake _____ cakes in all.

7. I mix everything in a _____ bowl.

8. Each cake has _____ frosting. The twins like that color!

B. Write an adjective to complete each sentence.

9. Tina has lots of vegetables. She makes a _____ salad with Angelo.

10. First, Tina gets _____ dandelions.

11. She washes the _____ leaves.

12. Then Angelo slices a _____ tomato.

13. It is from the _____ garden in our front yard.

14. The tomatoes grow on _____ plants.

C. Complete each sentence. Choose an adjective from the box.

crunchy	dirty	happy	hungry	safe	sweet

15. I am _____ to help Tina.

16. We add nuts to the salad. They are _____.

17. Next, I cut a fresh pear. It is _____.

18. A carrot is _____. Tina washes it.

19. Now everything in our salad is _____ to eat.

20. My family is _____ now. We all want to eat.

D. Complete each sentence. Use an adjective.

21. We cook well together. I am _____.

22. Luisa wants to learn more about unusual foods. She is _____.

23. "I love to eat chicken feet," says Tina. "They are _____."

24. Carlos says, "Try a fried ant. It is _____."

25. We won't eat bugs today. I am _____ about that!

Use Adjectives That Compare

- You can use an **adjective** to make a comparison.

   Joel is not as **old** as Diego.

- You can also change the form of the adjective to make the comparison.

   Add **-er** to short adjectives to compare two people, places, or things.

old + -er = older	Diego is **older**.
tall + -er = taller	Joel is **taller**.

- Often, you will use the word **than** after the adjective.

   Diego is older **than** Joe. Joe is taller **than** Diego.

Try It

A. Compare people and things in your classroom. Use the sentence builder to write three sentences.

_____	is are	shorter older taller	than	_____.

1. _____

2. _____

3. _____

B. Complete each sentence. Use the correct adjective.

4. Joel's arms are _____ than Diego's arms.

long/longer

5. Diego's legs are _____ than Joel's legs.

short/shorter

6. Diego is _____ on the basketball court than Joel.

fast/faster

43 Use an Adjective + -*er* to Compare

Do you want to compare two things? Just add **-er** to a short **adjective**. The word **than** usually comes after the adjective.

old + -er = older

Adjective	Adjective That Compares	Example
short	**shorter**	Sean is **shorter** than Tim.
light	**lighter**	Tim's hair is **lighter** than Sean's hair.

Tim's character is **older** than Sean's character.

Try It

A. Add -er to the adjective. Then complete the sentence with the adjective that compares.

1. dark _____

Sean's beard is _____ than Tim's beard.

2. long _____

Tim's lines are _____ than Sean's lines.

3. loud _____

Tim's voice is _____ than Sean's voice.

B. Complete each sentence with an adjective from the box. Make the adjective compare.

soft	tall	young

4. Tim is _____ than Sean.

5. Sean's character in the play is _____ than Tim's character.

6. Sean's voice is _____ than Tim's voice.

44 Use *More* + an Adjective to Compare

Some **adjectives** are long words. For long adjectives, use the word **more** to compare two things.

more + **graceful** = **more graceful**

Adjective	Adjective That Compares	Example
graceful	more graceful	Carla is **more graceful** than Jan.
energetic	more energetic	Jan is **more energetic** than Carla.
cheerful	more cheerful	Jan is also **more cheerful** than Carla.

Try It

A. Add **more** before the adjective. Then write the sentence with the adjective that compares.

1. athletic _____

Jan is _____ than Carla.

2. thoughtful _____

Carla is _____ than Jan.

3. confident _____

Carla is also _____ .

B. Complete each sentence. Use the adjective in parentheses. Make each adjective compare.

4. Jan is _____ than Carla. **(active)**

5. Carla's strokes are _____ than Jan's strokes. **(graceful)**

6. Carla's form is also _____ . **(beautiful)**

45 Use Adjectives That Compare

- Use an **adjective** to compare two people, places, or things.

1. If the adjective is short, add **-er**.	**bright**	**clear**	**soft**
	brighter	**clearer**	**softer**
2. If the adjective is long, use **more** before the adjective.	**wonderful**		**creative**
	more wonderful		**more creative**

- Never use **-er** and **more** together.

  Marta's painting is more brighter than Jorge's painting.

  Jorge's painting is more beautifuler than Marta's painting.

Try It

A. Cross out -er or more. Write the new sentence.

1. Marta's paintings are more cheerfuler than Jorge's paintings. _____

_____

2. His colors are more darker than Marta's colors. _____

_____

3. Marta's artwork is more softer than Jorge's artwork. _____

_____

4. Marta is more skillfuler than Jorge. _____

B. Complete each sentence. Use the adjective in parentheses. Make the adjective compare.

5. Jorge's portraits are _____ than Marta's portraits. **(powerful)**

6. Marta's portraits are _____ than Jorge's portraits. **(calm)**

7. Marta's landscapes are _____ than Jorge's landscapes. **(creative)**

8. However, Jorge's colors are _____ than Marta's colors. **(beautiful)**

46 Use an Adjective + -*est* to Compare

Do you want to compare three or more things? Just add **-est** to a short **adjective**. The word **the** always comes before an adjective that ends with **-est**.

strong + **-est** = **strongest**

Adjective	Adjective That Compares	Example
strong	strongest	Laura has **the strongest** legs of all the team members.
long	longest	She takes **the longest** steps of all.

Try It

A. Add **-est** to the adjective. Then write the sentence with the adjective that compares.

1. short _____

Olga has the _____ legs of all the runners.

2. quick _____

She is the _____ in short races, though.

3. old _____

Laura is the _____ member of the team.

B. Complete each sentence with an adjective from the box. Make the adjective compare.

new	short	young

4. Olga is the _____ runner on the team.

5. She also takes the _____ steps.

6. Marianna is the _____ member of the team.

47 Use *Most* + an Adjective to Compare

Some **adjectives** are long words. For long adjectives, use the word **most** to compare three or more things.

most + **humorous** = **most humorous**

Adjective	Adjective That Compares	Example
serious	most serious	Kylie is the **most serious** of the friends.
cheerful	most cheerful	Nicki is the **most cheerful**.

Serena is the **most humorous** of them all.

Try It

A. Add **most** before the adjective. Then write the sentence with the adjective that compares.

1. **talkative** _____

   Serena is also the _____ one in the group.

2. **carefree** _____

   Nicki is the _____ of the friends.

3. **unselfish** _____

   She is also the _____ of them.

4. **generous** _____

   In fact, Nicki is the _____ person in the restaurant.

B. Complete each sentence. Use the adjective in parentheses. Make the adjective compare.

5. Kylie is the _____ one in the group. **(sensitive)**

6. She says the _____ things. **(thoughtful)**

7. Serena is the _____ of the friends. **(artistic)**

8. She has the _____ ideas of all. **(unusual)**

48 Use Irregular Adjectives to Compare

- These **adjectives** have special forms.

To Describe 1 Thing	good	bad
To Compare 2 Things	better	worse
To Compare 3 or More Things	best	worst

- How many things are being compared here?

    Taye has a **better** idea than I have.

    Andrew has the **best** idea of all.

Try It

A. Complete each sentence with the correct adjective.

1. Ethan has a good idea for raising money, but Andrew's idea is _____ than
    better/best
    Ethan's idea.

2. The _____ idea of all is to play a funny soccer game.
    better/best

3. I can pretend to be the _____ soccer player ever.
    worse/worst

4. I can be _____ than someone who doesn't know the game at all.
    worse/worst

B. Complete each sentence. Use the correct form of the adjective in parentheses.

5. People will laugh at the _____ game in the world. **(bad)**

6. That is the _____ way of all to raise money for our team. **(good)**

7. That idea is _____ than having a bake sale. **(good)**

8. Sometimes a popular idea is _____ than a new idea. **(bad)**

Use Adjectives That Compare

To compare two things:

- Add **-er** to many **adjectives**.

  This basketball court is **newer** than my old court.

- Use **more** before long adjectives.

  My new teammates are **more athletic** than my old teammates.

- The word **than** usually comes after the adjective.

To compare three or more things:

- Add **-est** to many **adjectives**.

  This is the **newest** court in the city.

- Use **the most** before long adjectives.

  My new team is **the most athletic** team of all.

Try It

A. Complete each sentence with the correct form of the adjective in parentheses. Make the adjective compare.

1. Rasheed is on my new team. He is a _____
   player than I am. **(fast)**

2. He is also _____ at shooting baskets than I am. **(skillful)**

3. My new team scores a _____ number of points
   than my old team does. **(high)**

4. This team is _____ than my old team. **(powerful)**

5. The players are _____ than my old teammates. **(tough)**

6. Most of them are _____ than I am. **(confident)**

7. The coach is a _____ speaker than my old coach is. **(forceful)**

8. He is also the _____ coach I know. **(strict)**

B. Choose an adjective from the box to complete each sentence. Make the adjectives compare.

comfortable	strong	talented	young

9. These players are _____ than my old teammates, too.

10. Rasheed is _____ than I am.

11. But Rasheed is _____ than I am.

12. I am _____ on this team now than before.

C. Complete each sentence with the correct form of the adjective.

13. Rasheed is the _____ player in my school.
    famousest / most famous

14. He is the _____ player in the whole city.
    fastest / most fast

15. He plays the _____ games ever.
    excitingest / most exciting

16. He is the _____ player on the team.
    valuablest / most valuable

D. Rewrite each sentence to compare with **-est** or **most**. Add other words as needed.

17. Basketball is a popular game in my town. _____

_____

18. Basketball players are incredible athletes. _____

_____

19. My teammates win tough games. _____

_____

20. Rasheed has a bright future. _____

_____

Use Possessive Nouns

Use a **possessive noun** to show that someone owns or has something. To form a possessive with singular nouns, add **'s** to the end of the noun.

Jayden's guitar is new.

Nadia's friend wants to play the guitar.

She wants to play **Miguel's** drums, too.

Try It

A. Choose a noun from the box to complete each sentence. Make the noun show possession.

Harry	Jodi	Mr. Delmar	Mrs. Green	Victor

1. _____ father works in a music store.

2. _____ customer wants to buy a guitar.

3. This guitar is perfect for _____ daughter.

4. Lynn asks for _____ advice about music.

5. _____ mom buys the music.

B. Write a possessive noun to complete the second sentence in each pair.

6. Tony has an old piano. _____ piano is old.

7. That guitar belongs to Jesse. That is _____ guitar.

8. Heather has a goal. _____ goal is to sing.

9. Grandma sings pretty songs. I like to listen to _____ songs.

10. Leo sings with friends. _____ friends sing.

49 Use Possessive Nouns for One Owner

- Use a **possessive noun** to show that someone owns or has something.

- Sometimes one person or thing has something. Add **'s** to the end of the noun.

One Owner	Add **'s**	Sentence
the band of **Ryan**	**Ryan's** band	**Ryan's** band is a rock band.
the music of the **boy**	the **boy's** music	The band plays the **boy's** music.

Try It

A. Rewrite the underlined words to include a possessive noun.

1. The <u>practice of the band</u> is every Saturday. _____

2. The band practices in <u>the garage of Leah.</u> _____

3. The <u>voice of the singer</u> is beautiful. _____

4. Did you go to <u>the concert of the group</u>? _____

B. Rewrite each sentence to include a possessive noun.

5. The friends of Lisa are band members. _____

6. Pedro is the drummer of the band. _____

7. I like the music of Pedro. _____

8. He plays to the beat of the music. _____

50 Use Possessive Nouns for More Than One Owner

- Use a **possessive noun** to show that people own or have something.

- Sometimes more than one person or thing has something. Add **'** to the end of the noun if the noun ends in **-s**. Add **'s** if the noun does not end in **-s**.

More Than One Owner	Add ' or 's	Sentence
the team of the **boys**	the **boys'** team	The **boys'** team is in a race.
the team of the **women**	the **women's** team	The **women's** team runs, too.

Try It

A. Rewrite the underlined words to include a possessive noun.

1. The race of the men is starting. _____

2. The cheers of the people are loud. _____

3. The crowd watches the students of the coaches. _____

4. The smiles of the winners are huge! _____

B. Rewrite each sentence to include a possessive noun.

5. The race of the runners is over. _____

6. The legs of the students are tired. _____

7. The parents of the children are proud. _____

8. The buses of the schools are waiting to take the tired runners home. _____

_____

51 Use Possessive Nouns

Use a **possessive noun** to show who owns or has something.

One Owner	Add **'s**	One **girl's** painting shows swimmers.
More Than One Owner	Add **'** if the noun ends in **-s**.	These **students'** paintings show animals.
	Add **'s** if the noun does not end in **-s**.	Hana paints some **people's** pets.

Try It

A. Rewrite the underlined words to include a possessive noun.

1. The goal of Hana is to be a painter. _____

2. She paints pictures for the art show of the school. _____

3. The paintings of her classmates have bright colors. _____

4. This painting shows a playground of children! _____

B. Rewrite each sentence to include a possessive noun.

5. The painting of that teen shows a swimming race. _____

_____

6. The bathing suits of the swimmers are red and yellow. _____

_____

7. The bathing caps of the women are green and blue. _____

_____

8. I like the paintings of the artists. _____

52 Use Possessive Adjectives: My, Your, His, Her, and Its

A **possessive adjective** tells who owns or has something.

I ⟶ **my**	I am Felipe. Myra is **my** sister.
you ⟶ **your**	Do you have a sister? Who is **your** sister?
he ⟶ **his**	Mr. Debarge is the teacher. He teaches **his** students.
she ⟶ **her**	Myra is a dancer. She dances in **her** recital.
it ⟶ **its**	It is a fun recital. **Its** dancers are wonderful.

Try It

A. Write the correct word to complete each sentence.

1. I watch _____ sister's recital.
   I / my

2. _____ recital is at the new Arts Center.
   She / Her

3. _____ stage is good for ballet.
   Its / It

B. Write a possessive adjective to complete each sentence.

4. The dancers are happy. _____ recital is over.

5. "You were really great. I love _____ dancing!" I tell Myra.

6. My dad gives _____ daughter a big hug.

53 Use Possessive Adjectives: *Our*, *Your*, and *Their*

A **possessive adjective** tells who owns or has something.

we ⟶ **our**	We play tennis. **Our** team is good.
you ⟶ **your**	Do you both play tennis? Are you both on **your** school team?
they ⟶ **their**	The players practice. They bring **their** tennis racquets.

Try It

A. Write the correct word to complete each sentence.

1. My brothers play tennis. Tennis is _____ favorite sport.
   they / their

2. We play tennis every day. _____ goal is to get better.
   We / Our

3. You both can play, too. Bring _____ racquets.
   your / you

4. We practice _____ serves today.
   our / your

5. Watch those players. _____ serves are good.
   Their / Our

B. Write a possessive adjective to complete each sentence.

6. We have a tennis match today. We think _____ team is ready.

7. The players on the other team are good. _____ team has not lost a match yet.

8. "You all have done _____ best at practice," Coach Ruiz says.

9. The other players are ready. They will try _____ hardest to win.

10. We are ready, too. _____ goal is to win!

54 Use Possessive Adjectives

- A **possessive adjective** tells who owns or has something.

  Jamal plays basketball. It is **his** favorite sport.

- Use the correct possessive adjective to show who owns something.

Subject Pronouns	I	you	he	she	it	we	they
Possessive Adjectives	my	your	his	her	its	our	their

Try It

A. **Complete each sentence. Write the correct possessive adjective.**

1. Jamal plays basketball in high school. _____ dream is to play in college, too.
   My / His

2. Many basketball players are tall. _____ height helps them reach the basket.
   Their / Your

3. Jamal is tall. He can touch the basket. He jumps up and hits _____ rim.
   their / its

4. I play basketball, too. Jamal is on _____ team.
   my / her

5. Both of us are good players. We help _____ team win.
   its / our

B. **Write a possessive adjective to complete each sentence.**

6. Mom likes to watch me play basketball. She goes to all of _____ games.

7. She cheers for all of us players. She claps when _____ shots go in.

8. Mom is proud of me. She tells everyone that I am _____ son.

9. "You played well tonight. _____ game was the best yet," Mom tells me.

10. The players all like Mom. They say Mom is _____ biggest fan.

Use Possessive Adjectives

A **possessive adjective** tells who someone or something belongs to.

I ——→ **my**	**I** have a dream. **My** dream is to be a doctor.
you ——→ **your**	Do **you** have a dream? What is **your** dream?
he ——→ **his**	Omar plays soccer. **He** is the captain of **his** team.
she ——→ **her**	Allison writes. **She** works for **her** town newspaper.
it ——→ **its**	**It** is a good newspaper. **Its** stories are interesting.
we ——→ **our**	**We** all have **our** own dreams.
you ——→ **your**	Will **you** two share **your** dreams with the class?
they ——→ **their**	**They** hope **their** dreams come true.

Match the possessive adjective to the noun or pronoun it goes with.

Omar scores a goal for **his** team.

We cheer for **our** school team.

Try It

A. Complete each sentence. Write the correct word.

1. I want _____ dream to become a doctor to come true.

my / I

2. Mrs. Berg teaches science. I am in _____ class.

she / her

3. We all work hard on _____ science labs.

we / our

4. Dr. Berg comes in to talk about _____ job.

he / his

5. Doctors know that _____ jobs are important.

their / they

B. Complete each sentence. Write the correct possessive adjective.

6. Omar wants to play soccer. That is _____ dream.
<u>their / his</u>

7. Omar plays in a summer soccer league. _____ players come from all over
<u>Its / Your</u>
the city.

8. They practice _____ soccer skills every day.
<u>my / their</u>

9. One coach asks Omar, "Did you practice _____ kicking yesterday?"
<u>her / your</u>

10. Omar answers, "I think _____ kicking skills have improved."
<u>my / its</u>

C. Complete each sentence. Write the correct word.

11. Allison loves to write. _____ dream is to be a writer.
<u>She / Her</u>

12. _____ think Allison writes great articles.
<u>I / My</u>

13. "_____ articles are interesting to read, Allison," everyone always says.
<u>You / Your</u>

14. Mr. Marquez is Allison's teacher. _____ writing class is really hard.
<u>He / His</u>

15. _____ is a wonderful class, though.
<u>It / Its</u>

16. "_____ teacher teaches the best class," the writing students say.
<u>We / Our</u>

D. Complete each sentence. Write the correct possessive adjective.

17. The students tell about _____ dreams.

18. Abigail says _____ dream is to be a veterinarian.

19. Abigail has three cats. "I take good care of _____ cats," she says.

20. Rico wants to be a concert pianist. He practices on _____ piano every day.

21. You must have _____ own dreams.

22. We all believe in _____ dreams.

✓ Check Apostrophes in Possessive Nouns

A **possessive noun** tells who or what owns something. When you use a possessive noun in writing, be sure to include an apostrophe (**'**).

One Owner	Add **'s**.	**Nyla's** baseball team is very good.
More Than One Owner	Add **'** if the noun ends in **-s**. Add **'s** if the noun does not end in **-s**.	The **players'** skills improve each week. The team plays in a **women's** league.

Try It

A. Complete each sentence. Write the phrase in parentheses as a possessive noun.

1. _____ has a game every Saturday. (**The team of Nyla**)

2. _____ are blue and white. (**The uniforms of the players**)

3. _____ is a bluebird. (**The symbol of the team**)

4. The team listens carefully to _____. (**the instructions of the coach**)

5. Each pitcher watches _____. (**the signals of the catcher**)

6. The batters hear _____. (**the cheers of the people**)

7. The fans applaud _____. (**the speed of the runners**)

B. (8–12) Edit the paragraph. Add or take out apostrophes where necessary.

Nyla's brother Owen likes baseball, too. Owens team is called the Jaguars'. The teams captain set a record last season. He hit the most runs of anyone in the mens league. The Jaguars coach is very proud.

Mark Your Changes

Add an apostrophe.
Tad is the team͜s pitcher.
Take out an apostrophe.
The mitts᾽ are leather.

✓ Check Your Spelling
Words That Sound Alike

Homonyms are words that sound alike but have different meanings and spellings. Make sure you are using the correct word.

Homonym and Its Meaning	Example Sentence
it's = it is; it has	**It's** time for the race to begin!
its = belonging to it	The track is ready. **Its** surface is smooth.
there = place or position	The runners are waiting over **there**.
their = belonging to them	They talk with **their** coaches.
they're = they are	**They're** listening and stretching.

Try It

A. Edit each sentence. Replace incorrect words.

1. The runners take there places on the start line.

2. Ten sprinters wait they're.

3. Their ready to run!

4. A horn blasts. Its very loud.

5. It's a long way around the track. It's lanes are narrow.

Mark Your Changes

Replace with this.
They're
~~There~~ running fast.

B. Complete each sentence. Use the correct word from the chart.

6. All the runners are fast. _____ legs are strong.

7. Soon _____ near the finish line.

8. A man with a stopwatch stands _____ .

9. The watch is ticking. _____ second hand moves quickly.

10. _____ a very close race!

✔ Check for Commas

- A good description includes describing words. Add a comma between two **adjectives** that come before a **noun**.

   Jake hit the **small** , **round** tennis **ball**.

- Do not add a comma if one of the adjectives is a number.

   His **two hard serves** went into the net.

Try It

A. **Edit each sentence. Add commas where necessary.**

1. The tall energetic player served again.

2. His low fast serve flew over the net.

3. The two talented boys played well.

4. They both received long loud applause after the match.

Mark Your Changes
Add a comma.
It was a long‸difficult match.

B. **Write four sentences about fans at a sports event. Use two adjectives from the box in each sentence. Remember to use commas where needed.**

disappointed	favorite	happy	hungry
loud	quiet	three	two

5. _____

   _____

6. _____

   _____

7. _____

   _____

8. _____

   _____

Use Adjectives Before Nouns

Remember: Adjectives are words that describe people, places, or things.

- **Adjectives** describe in many ways.

How something looks	green, golden, round, tall, tiny, long
How something sounds	noisy, loud, squeaky, quiet, musical, shrill
How something feels	smooth, sharp, rough, chilly, itchy, hot
How something tastes	delicious, salty, sweet, bitter, minty, sour
How many there are	one, five, twenty, few, some, many

- An **adjective** often comes before the **noun** it describes.
  I see **many delicious foods** in the lunchroom.

Try It

A. Complete each sentence. Write an adjective from the box.

hot   spicy   two

1. Pedro eats a _____ mix of chicken and beans.

2. He also has _____ rolls today. He gives me one!

3. I have some _____ soup. I need to wait till it cools.

B. Complete each sentence. Write an adjective and a noun from the box.

4. Tanisha opens a _____ .

5. She gives us each a handful of _____ .

6. "These make a _____ .
They are vegetables!"

Adjectives	Nouns
yummy	**bag**
crunchy	**snack**
large	**chips**

Use Adjectives That Compare

Remember: You can use an adjective to make a comparison.

- Use an adjective to compare two people, places, or things. Add **-er** to a short adjective. Use **more** before a long adjective. Never use **-er** and **more** together.

    My neighborhood is **older** than your neighborhood.

    It is **more historic** than your neighborhood, too.

- Use an adjective to compare three or more people, places, or things. Add **-est** to a short adjective. Use **most** before a long adjective. Never use **-est** and **most** together.

    I live in the **oldest** neighborhood in the city.

    It is in the **most historic** part of town.

Try It

A. Complete each sentence. Write the correct adjective.

1. Dad works in the _____ building in the city.

most tallest / tallest

2. His job seems _____ than before.

harder / more harder

3. He enjoys this _____ and bigger office, though.

newer / newest

4. I think big cities are the _____ places to live and work.

more wonderful / most wonderful

5. Of course, I live in the _____ city anywhere!

gloriousest / most glorious

B. Complete each sentence. Use the adjective in parentheses. Make the adjective compare.

6. Maria lives in a _____ town than mine. **(small)**

7. She calls it the _____ place around. **(beautiful)**

8. The people are _____ than the people I know. **(cheerful)**

9. The streets are _____ in her town, too. **(quiet)**

10. Maria says, "It is the _____ place to live of all." **(pleasant)**

Use Possessive Nouns

Remember: A possessive noun shows that someone owns or has something.

Sometimes one person or thing owns or has something. To form a singular **possessive noun**, add **'s** to the end of the noun.

One Owner	Add 's	Sentence
the team of **Zak**	**Zak's** team	**Zak's** team makes a robot.
the job of the **robot**	the **robot's** job	The **robot's** job is to throw a ball.

Try It

A. **Rewrite each sentence. Use a possessive noun to replace the underlined words.**

1. The interest of Javier is programming. _____

2. He and Zak write the programs of the robot. _____
   _____

3. The group of Stella puts all the wires in the robot. _____
   _____

4. They get help from the mother of Vi. _____

5. On this project, the job of each group is important. _____
   _____

B. **Complete the sentences. Use possessive adjectives.**

REMEMBER
- A **possessive adjective** tells who owns or has something.
- **My, your, his, her, its, our,** and **their** are possessive adjectives.

6. Anita works hard. _____ work helps the team.

7. David knows a lot. _____ knowledge helps, too.

8. These students all work hard to finish _____ robot.

9. The robot works! All of _____ shots go into the basket.

10. The students say, "We are proud of _____ robot."

Use Past Tense Verbs With *-ed*

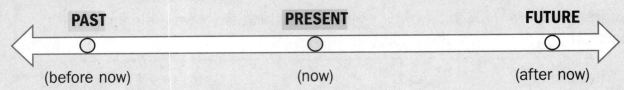

The **tense**, or time, of a **verb** shows when an action happens.

PAST   **PRESENT**   **FUTURE**

(before now)   (now)   (after now)

- A verb in the **present tense** says what happens now or often.
  Right now, clouds **fill** the sky.
- A verb in the **past tense** says what happened before now.
  Yesterday, clouds **filled** the sky.
- Add **-ed** to most verbs when you say what happened in the past.
  turn + **-ed** = turn**ed**   start + **-ed** = start**ed**
  The sky **turned** gray. The wind **started** to blow.

Try It

A. Change the <u>verb</u> to the past tense. Then write the sentence in the
past tense.

1. Strong winds <u>lift</u> my hat from my head. _____

_____

2. A flowerpot <u>crashes</u> to the ground. _____

_____

3. My cat <u>jumps</u> out of the way just in time. _____

_____

B. Write the correct verb to complete the sentence.

4. Yesterday, the wind _____ all day long.
                         howls / howled

5. Last night, I _____ a tree fall into the street.
                   watch / watched

6. After the storm, people _____ the mess out of their yards.
                         clean / cleaned

55 Use Past Tense Verbs

- The **tense** of a **verb** shows when an action happens.
- Action in the **present tense** happens now or often.
- Action in the **past tense** happened before now.

PAST	PRESENT	FUTURE
(before now)	(now)	(after now)

- Add **-ed** to most verbs when you talk or write about what happened in the past.

    look + **-ed** = look**ed**   start + **-ed** = start**ed**

1. I **look** at the sky.   **2.** It **starts** to snow.

    Yesterday, I **looked** at the sky.   Yesterday, it **started** to snow.

Try It

A. Complete each sentence. Write the past tense of the verb in parentheses.

1. Yesterday, the weather forecaster _____ about the storm. **(talk)**

2. She _____ more than two feet of snow. **(predict)**

3. I _____ a day off from school. **(expect)**

4. Then it _____ all night! **(snow)**

B. Complete each sentence. Choose a verb from the box. Write it in the past tense.

show	stay	turn	watch

5. Early this morning we _____ on the news channel.

6. TV reporters _____ pictures of the snow.

7. My family _____ home from work and school.

8. We _____ the blizzard from inside our warm, safe house.

56 Spell Past Tense Verbs Correctly

- Sometimes you can just add **-ed** to the verb to form the past tense.

  Snow start**ed** to fall very hard. **(start)**

  My family stay**ed** inside, safe and warm. **(stay)**

- Other times, you have to change the spelling of the verb before you add **-ed**.
  If a verb ends in silent **e**, drop the **e**. Then add **-ed**.

  We huddl**ed** by the fire. **(huddle)**

  Then I notic**ed** an empty dog bed. Where was Dusty? **(notice)**

Try It

A. Complete each sentence. Write the past tense of the verb in parentheses.

1. I _____ the front door. **(open)**

2. A blast of snow _____ me. **(surprise)**

3. Again and again, I _____ Dusty's name. **(shout)**

4. Dusty didn't come. Sadly, I _____ the door. **(close)**

B. Complete each sentence. Choose a verb from the box. Write it in the past tense.

arrive	hope	open	scratch	search	survive

5. We _____ the house.

6. I _____ to find Dusty safe.

7. Soon the end of the storm _____ .

8. Something _____ against my bedroom door.

9. I _____ the door. I didn't believe my eyes.

10. Dusty _____ . She was under my bed the entire time!

57 Spell Past Tense Verbs Correctly

- Sometimes you can just add -**ed** to the verb to form the past tense.
  Clara plow**ed** the snow off the driveway. **(plow)**
  Felix help**ed**. **(help)**

- Other times, you have to change the spelling of the verb before you add -**ed**. Some one-syllable verbs end in one vowel and one consonant. Double the consonant before you add -**ed**.
  Felix slipp**ed** on the ice. **(slip)**
  He dropp**ed** his shovel. **(drop)**

Try It

A. Complete each sentence. Write the past tense of the verb in parentheses.

1. Felix _____ hard onto the ice. **(slam)**

2. His ankle _____ . **(twist)**

3. Clara raced over. She _____ Felix. **(grab)**

4. She carefully _____ him stand up. **(help)**

5. With her help, Felix _____ to the house. **(hop)**

B. Complete each sentence. Choose a verb from the box. Write it in the past tense.

call	nod	rest	stop	wrap

6. Mom _____ her work.

7. She _____ a bandage around Felix's ankle.

8. Felix _____ his ankle.

9. Clara _____ her head. "Good job!" she said.

10. She _____ a neighbor to borrow some crutches.

58 Use *Was* and *Were* in Statements

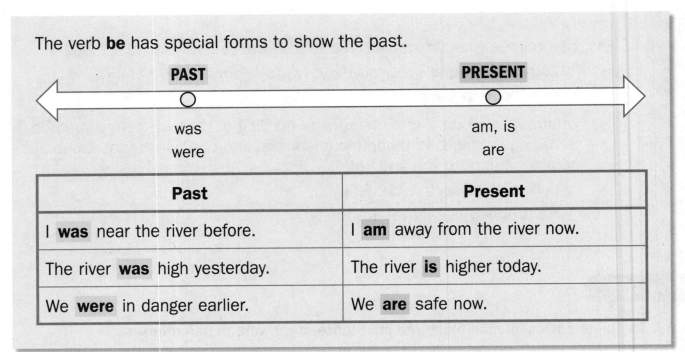

The verb **be** has special forms to show the past.

PAST ○ ←————————————→ ○ PRESENT

was
were

am, is
are

Past	Present
I **was** near the river before.	I **am** away from the river now.
The river **was** high yesterday.	The river **is** higher today.
We **were** in danger earlier.	We **are** safe now.

Try It

A. Rewrite each sentence. Use the past tense of the <u>verb</u>.

1. River water <u>is</u> everywhere. _____

2. Some cars <u>are</u> under the water. _____

3. Many basements <u>are</u> full of water. _____

4. My neighborhood <u>is</u> a mess. _____

5. My family <u>is</u> very upset. _____

B. Write the correct verb to complete each sentence.

6. Yesterday, I _____ afraid.
   _{am / was}

7. Last night, we _____ in a motel.
   _{are / were}

8. By midnight last night, the flood _____ over.
   _{is / was}

9. By this morning, we _____ ready to go home.
   _{are / were}

10. Now people _____ busy with cleanup.
    _{are / were}

59 Use *Was* and *Were* in Questions

- Use **was** or **were** to ask questions about something that happened in the past.

- In the question, put the **subject** after the **verb was** or **were**.

- In the answer, put the **subject** before **was** or **were**.

Was the **family** safe after the storm?

Question	Answer
Was the **water** in your house?	Yes, the **water was** in our house.
Were the **streets** underwater?	Yes, **they were**.
Where **were you and your family**?	**We were** at a shelter.

Try It

A. Put the words in the right order to ask a question. Then write an answer to the question.

1. the flood water / dirty / Was / ? _____

2. over / When / the storm / was / ? _____

3. was / the damage / What / ? _____

4. Were / in this neighborhood / safe / people / ? _____

_____

B. Read each answer. Then write a question for it.

5. The big flood was last week. _____

6. Yes, power lines were on the ground. _____

7. The water was in the basement. _____

8. Yes, all the neighbors were safe. _____

60 Use *Was* and *Were* in Negative Statements

- Use **was** or **were** with **not** to make a negative statement about the past.
- Put **not** after the **verb**.

1. Grandpa **was** afraid of the storm.

   Grandpa **was** **not** afraid of the storm.

2. My great-aunts **were** upstairs.

   My great-aunts **were** **not** upstairs.

Try It

A. Add **not** to make each statement negative. Write the negative statement.

1. My grandparents were alone during the storm. _____

   _____

2. My great-aunt was here at the start of the storm. _____

   _____

3. Grandma's friends were outside in the rain. _____

   _____

4. Their stories about the storm were scary. _____

   _____

B. Write the words in the correct order to make a negative statement.

5. were / My grandparents / not outside / on a windy day / . _____

   _____

6. not / was / The tornado / near Grandma's house / . _____

   _____

7. here / during that big storm / not / My relatives / were / . _____

   _____

8. not / The big storm / was / a blizzard / . _____

Use Past Tense Verbs: *Was, Were*

When you talk about the past, you usually use past tense verbs.

The verb **be** has two special forms for the past: **was** and **were**.

- Use **was** with **I**, **he**, **she**, and **it**.
- Use **were** with **we**, **you**, and **they**.

The verbs agree, or go, with their subjects.

> I **was** at the movies.
> Helga **was** there, too.
> We **were** there together.
> The movies **were** about survivors.

Try It

A. Write the correct verb to complete each sentence.

1. One woman _____ a survivor of the hurricane.
   was / were

2. The hurricane _____ an awful storm.
   was / were

3. The winds _____ really strong.
   was / were

4. They _____ more than 100 miles per hour.
   was / were

5. That storm _____ one of the worst ever.
   was / were

6. The people _____ lucky to be alive.
   was / were

7. The houses on their street _____ not okay.
   was / were

8. Many survivors _____ homeless after the storm.
   was / were

9. Many pets _____ all alone.
   was / were

10. The damage _____ terrible.
    was / were

B. **(11–18)** Write **was** or **were** to complete the paragraph.

In one movie, people _____ survivors of a shipwreck. They _____ on an island, far from everything. The weather _____ hot. Food _____ hard to find. The survivors _____ brave, though. Two women _____ eager to help. Their idea _____ to start a fire. The smoke _____ a signal. Soon, rescuers found them!

C. Write each sentence in the past tense.

19. My family is in a mountain cave. _____

20. I am really afraid. _____

21. Rescuers are all around, though. _____

22. One rescuer is at the opening to the cave. _____

_____

23. My family is very happy. _____

24. We are survivors! _____

D. Complete each sentence. Use **was** or **were** and other words.

25. Last year, Lynn survived a storm. The storm _____ .

26. She told us about it. We _____ .

27. Yesterday, Jerry read about survivors. They _____ .

28. I remember a bad storm. It _____ .

29. My family went to the basement. We _____ .

30. We looked out the basement window. The sky _____ .

Use Past Tense Verbs: *Had*

- The verb **have** has a special form to tell about the past.

PAST	PRESENT	FUTURE
(before now)	(now)	(after now)

Past	Present
Last night, I **had** a problem.	Today, I still **have** a problem.
We **had** a hurricane.	We **have** a tree on the roof now.
My house **had** no power.	My house still **has** no power.
The rooms **had** no lights.	The rooms still **have** no lights.
My brother **had** work to do.	Now Dad **has** a big cleanup job.
My sister **had** an idea.	Mom **has** a lot to do, too.

- In the **past tense**, use **had** with all subjects.
- In the **present tense**, use **has** with **he**, **she**, and **it**. Use **have** with **I**, **you**, **we**, and **they**.

Try It

A. **(1–4) Complete each sentence. Write the correct verb.**

My sister _____ homework. Yesterday, she _____ time to
         have / has   has / had

finish it. We _____ lights then, too. Now we _____ no electricity.
         have / had   have / had

B. **Write have, has, or had to complete each sentence.**

5. My flashlight _____ no batteries yesterday.

6. Today, I _____ new batteries for it.

61 Use Irregular Verbs: *Did*

- The verb **do** has a special form to tell about the past.

PAST   PRESENT   FUTURE

(before now)   (now)   (after now)

Past	Present
Yesterday, Allen **did** a great job on the trail.	Today, Anita **does** cleanup to help Allen.
Many people **did** different jobs to help him.	She and her friends **do** a good job.
I **did**, too.	I **do** a good job, too.

- In the **past tense**, use **did** with all subjects.
- In the **present tense**, use **does** with **he**, **she**, and **it**. Use **do** with **I**, **you**, **we**, and **they**.

Try It

A. Complete each sentence. Write the correct verb.

1. Allen _____ a lot of trail work to help hikers.
   do / does

2. We _____ lots of projects together.
   do / did

3. Yesterday, we _____ a trail project together.
   do / did

4. After that, Allen _____ another project.
   does / did

B. Complete the sentences. Use **do**, **does**, or **did**.

5. Marta, look at those trail markers. Allen _____ some work earlier to place them.

6. I _____ a lot to help him with that job.

62 Use Irregular Verbs: *Brought, Made, Took*

- Add **-ed** to most verbs to show that an action already happened.
- Some verbs have a special form for the past tense. These verbs are **irregular verbs**.

Present	Past	Example in the Past
bring, brings	**brought**	We **brought** food on the camping trip.
make, makes	**made**	Monica **made** dinner over the campfire.
take, takes	**took**	Mom **took** her guitar and sang.

Try It

A. Rewrite each sentence. Use the past tense form of the <u>verb</u>.

1. It <u>takes</u> creative ideas to survive in the woods. _____

_____

2. Monica always <u>brings</u> plastic bags in her backpack. _____

_____

3. Sometimes Monica's actions <u>make</u> her friends laugh. _____

_____

4. One day, they <u>bring</u> good luck. _____

B. Complete each sentence. Use the past tense form of **bring**, **make**, or **take**.

5. Yesterday's weather _____ a lot of rain to the campsite.

6. Monica _____ the plastic bags out of her pack.

7. She _____ a bottle out of one bag to catch rainwater.

8. She _____ raincoats out of the other bags.

63 Use Irregular Verbs: *Knew, Got, Told*

- Add **-ed** to most verbs to show that an action already happened.
- Some verbs have a special form for the past tense. These verbs are **irregular verbs**.

Present	Past	Example in the Past
know, knows	**knew**	Felipe **knew** a survival story.
get, gets	**got**	His dog Max **got** into trouble a few weeks ago.
tell, tells	**told**	Felipe **told** the story of the dog's rescue.

Try It

A. Rewrite each sentence. Use the past tense form of the <u>verb</u>.

1. Felipe <u>tells</u> about Max and the icy pond. _____

2. Max <u>gets</u> onto the ice. _____

3. Felipe <u>knows</u> about the dangers of ice. _____

4. He <u>gets</u> up close to the edge of the pond. _____

_____

5. He <u>tells</u> Max to come back. _____

B. Complete each sentence. Use the past tense form of **know**, **get**, or **tell**.

6. Felipe _____ the right thing to do.

7. He _____ his cell phone out of his pocket.

8. He _____ the 911 operator about his dog.

9. Firefighters quickly _____ Max to safety.

10. Max wagged his tail. Felipe _____ Max was glad to be safe.

64 Use Irregular Verbs: *Saw, Thought, Wrote*

- Add **-ed** to most verbs to show that an action already happened.
- Some verbs have a special form for the past tense. These verbs are **irregular verbs**.

Present	Past	Example in the Past
see, sees	**saw**	Tran **saw** great books at the library.
think, thinks	**thought**	"That's interesting!" she **thought**.
write, writes	**wrote**	Authors **wrote** many books about rescues.

Try It

A. **Rewrite each sentence. Use the past tense form of the <u>verb</u>.**

1. Two authors <u>write</u> about a rescue at sea. _____

_____

2. Tran <u>sees</u> a picture of what happened. Another boat saved all the people. _____

_____

3. Tran <u>thinks</u> about the scary event. _____

4. The people <u>think</u> about their luck. _____

B. **Complete each sentence. Use the past tense form of see, think, or write.**

5. Other authors _____ stories about rescues.

6. Tran _____ many photos in the stories.

7. She _____ about the people's courage.

8. Then Tran _____ an essay about her favorite story.

65 Use Irregular Verbs: *Met, Said, Felt*

- Add **-ed** to most verbs to show that an action already happened.
- Some verbs have a special form for the past tense. These verbs are **irregular verbs**.

Present	Past	Example in the Past
meet, meets	**met**	I **met** a special person yesterday.
say, says	**said**	He **said**, "I have a story to tell."
feel, feels	**felt**	I **felt** lucky to hear him speak.

Try It

A. Rewrite each sentence. Use the past tense form of the <u>verb</u>.

1. The speaker <u>says</u>, "I am a survivor of an earthquake." _____

   _____

2. He <u>feels</u> lucky because he survived. _____

3. Some students <u>meet</u> with him later. _____

4. We <u>say</u>, "We liked your speech. We learned a lot." _____

   _____

B. Complete each sentence. Use the past tense form of **meet**, **say**, or **feel**.

5. The speaker _____ afraid during the earthquake.

6. He _____ , "The ground shook hard."

7. "I _____ like I was on a roller coaster."

8. The survivors _____ at a shelter after the earthquake.

66 Use Irregular Verbs: *Found, Wore, Sat*

- Add **-ed** to most verbs to show that an action already happened.
- Some verbs have a special form for the past tense. These verbs are **irregular verbs**.

Present	Past	Example in the Past
find, finds	**found**	I **found** an old jacket yesterday.
wear, wears	**wore**	I **wore** it in our house. We did not have heat during the storm.
sit, sits	**sat**	We **sat** for hours in the cold house.

Try It

A.   Rewrite each sentence. Use the past tense form of the <u>verb</u>.

1.   My family <u>sits</u> in the dark. _____

2.   My brothers <u>find</u> a flashlight. _____

3.   I <u>wear</u> an old jacket and mittens. _____

4.   Mom <u>finds</u> a quilt to keep herself warm. _____

5.   My brother Jack <u>wears</u> a wool hat. _____

B.   Complete each sentence. Use the past tense form of find, wear, or sit.

6.   My dog _____ a way to help me.

7.   She _____ on my lap and took a nap.

8.   So I _____ my old jacket—and a furry coat, too!

9.   My dad _____ us in the dark.

10.   We _____ together until the power came back.

Use Irregular Past Tense Verbs

- We add **-ed** to most verbs to show that an action happened before now.

    The storm start**ed** last night.

- But, some verbs have a special form for the past tense. These verbs are irregular.

Present	Past	Example in the Past
come, comes	came	The winds **came** during the night.
do, does	did	They **did** a lot of damage.
go, goes	went	My family **went** to the basement.
have, has	had	We **had** a safe place there.
run, runs	ran	Our dog **ran** downstairs to be with us.

Try It

A. Change each verb in parentheses to the past tense. Write it to complete the sentence.

1. I _____ outside this morning. **(go)**

2. I _____ a huge surprise. **(have)**

3. Three branches from the oak tree _____ down last night. **(come)**

4. I _____ to get my parents. **(run)**

5. They _____ to look at the damage. **(come)**

6. Dad _____ a chainsaw in the garage. **(have)**

7. He _____ to get it right away. **(go)**

8. For the rest of the day, Dad _____ a lot of work. **(do)**

B. Write each sentence with the verb in the past tense.

9. We have many thunderstorms this week. _____

10. The storms come with little warning. _____

11. We go for hours without electricity. _____

12. I do some creative thinking. _____

13. I run to buy charcoal at the store. _____

14. We have a cookout for dinner! _____

C. Complete each sentence with a verb from the box. Use the past tense form of the verb.

come	do	go	have	run

15. Mia _____ outside after the rainstorm.

16. Then she _____ a strange thing.

17. She quickly _____ inside to get her camera.

18. A beautiful rainbow _____ across the sky.

19. Mia soon _____ many pictures of the rainbow.

D. Write the verb that correctly completes the sentence.

20. Yesterday, Daniel _____ a scary time.
    has / had

21. A tree branch _____ through his window.
    came / come

22. The branch _____ a lot of damage to the house.
    do / did

23. Daniel _____ to a friend's house last night.
    goes / went

24. Today, he _____ a big cleanup job!
    has / had

Use Commands

- Use a **statement** to tell something. End the statement with a period.

  The sky is dark.

- Ask a **question** to find out something. End the question with a question mark.

  Is a thunderstorm coming?

- Give a **command** to tell someone what to do. End most commands with a period.

Commands with Action Verbs	Commands with *Be*
Walk quickly.	**Be** careful.
Don't stay outside!	**Don't be** late.

- A command begins with a verb. The subject (**you**) is understood.

- When you tell someone not to do something, use **don't** before the verb.

- Use the main verb form. Don't add an **-s**.

Try It

A. Read each sentence. Add the punctuation mark. Then write **statement**, **question**, or **command**.

1. Why is the sky so dark _____

2. It is going to rain soon _____

3. Don't leave the car windows open _____

B. Write a word from the box to complete each command.

don't	find	go

4. _____ shelter from the storm.

5. _____ into the house if you see lightning.

6. _____ be afraid of the thunder.

67 Use Commands

- A **command** tells someone what to do. A command begins with a capital letter. Most commands end with a period.

  Listen to the fire alarm.

- Some commands express strong feeling. A strong command ends with an exclamation point.

  Pay attention right now!

- Some commands are polite. A polite command starts with the word **please**.

  Please follow my instructions.

Try It

A. Read each command. Add the punctuation mark that you think belongs at the end.

1. Don't stop for anything _____

2. Please walk quickly out the door _____

3. Be careful around that burning wood _____

4. Look at all those fire engines _____

B. Choose a word from the box to complete each command. Write the first word and a punctuation mark.

be	please	stand	walk

5. _____ here quietly for a few minutes _____

6. _____ back to the school now _____

7. _____ careful around all these cars _____

8. _____ hold the door open _____

(68) Use Exclamations and Statements

- An **exclamation** shows strong feeling. An exclamation begins with a capital letter and ends with an exclamation point.

    That hurricane was the worst storm ever**!**

- Not every sentence shows strong feeling. A **statement** tells something. It ends with a period.

    I know a lot about storms**.**

- Do not use exclamations all the time. Use them only to show strong feeling.

    Thunderstorms are very powerful**.**

    Lightning split that tree in half**!**

Try It

A. Read each sentence. Is it an exclamation or a statement? Add the punctuation mark that you think belongs at the end.

1. I rowed a boat on the pond _____

2. Suddenly, I heard the loudest thunder ever _____

3. I rowed to shore quickly _____

4. I raced inside _____

5. The weather was horrible _____

B. Complete each sentence so that it shows strong feeling.

6. Suddenly, lightning struck _____

_____

7. I was glad _____

_____

8. That lightning _____

_____

69 Use Adverbs That Tell How

- Use an **adverb** to describe a verb. Many adverbs end in **-ly**.

  The storm ended **quickly**.

- Adverbs add details to your writing. Some adverbs tell **how** something happens.

  Denise walked **slowly** into her house.

  "Walk **carefully**," said Mom.

Try It

A. Complete each sentence. Use an adverb from the box.

badly	brightly	crookedly	fearfully	sadly

1. The sun shone _____ after the storm.

2. The family entered the house _____.

3. The house was _____ damaged from the storm.

4. Denise _____ looked around.

5. Pictures hung _____ on the walls.

B. Complete each sentence. Use an adverb that tells *how*.

6. Denise walked _____ into her room.

7. She stood _____ for a minute.

8. Just then, her cat _____ gave a "meow."

9. Denise shouted _____.

10. The cat _____ survived the storm.

70 Use Adverbs That Tell When

- Use an **adverb** to describe a verb. Adverbs add details to your writing.
- Some adverbs tell **when** something happens.

    A speaker came to school **yesterday**.

    She got our attention **immediately**.

Try It

A. Complete each sentence. Use an adverb from the box.

always	finally	first	next	soon	then

1. The speaker talked _____ about fear.

2. _____, she explained responses to fear.

3. Our bodies _____ have a fight or flight response.

4. I get frightened. I breathe faster _____.

5. _____, my heart beats faster, too.

6. _____, I fight—or I flee.

B. Complete each sentence. Use an adverb that tells *when*.

7. _____, I learned a lesson about fear from the speaker.

8. I did not know these things _____.

9. _____ I feel afraid.

10. _____ I know what to do when I am afraid.

11. I will _____ remember that speaker.

12. I will _____ forget about fight or flight.

71 Use Adverbs That Tell Where

- Use an **adverb** to describe a verb. Adverbs bring life to your writing.
- Some adverbs tell **where** something happens.
  "Look **outside**," I said.
  Snow fell **everywhere**.

Try It

A. Complete each sentence. Use an adverb from the box.

around	down	everywhere	inside	outside	somewhere

1. I stood _____.

2. Snow fell _____.

3. A snowplow worked _____, but I did not see it.

4. "Look _____, Grandpa," I said. "Everything is white."

5. "The plows piled snow _____."

6. Even more snow came _____ that night.

B. Complete each sentence. Use an adverb that tells *where*.

7. We went _____ the next morning.

8. Grandpa called, "Come _____, Raul."

9. "Let's dig _____. We can measure the snow."

10. Later we took a walk, but we did not go _____.

11. We looked _____ at all the snowy trees.

12. "Look _____! Someone made a snowman," I said.

72 Use the Adverb *Not*

- The word **not** is an **adverb**. You can add **not** to make a statement negative.
- If a statement has the verb **am**, **is**, **are**, **was**, or **were**, put **not** after the verb.

  1. Lena **is** afraid.

  Lena **is not** afraid.

  2. We **were** home alone.

  We **were not** home alone.

- For **action verbs**, put **not** between **did** or **does** and the action verb. Do not add **-ed** to the action verb.

  3. Something **crashed** to the floor.

  Something **did not crash** to the floor.

  4. The noise shocks Lena.

  The noise **does not shock** Lena.

Try It

A. **Make each statement negative. Write the negative statement.**

1. Lena walked over after the storm. _____

_____

2. Strange sounds in the house were a surprise to us. _____

_____

3. The noises ended suddenly. _____

_____

4. Lena wanted to explore. _____

_____

B. **Make negative statements. Use the verb in parentheses and the adverb not.**

5. We looked for the cause of the sounds. I _____ nervous. **(was)**

6. We _____ anything strange. The television was on! **(discover)**

Use Adverbs

- An **adverb** often describes a verb. An adverb can tell how, when, or where.

  We were in an earthquake **yesterday**. (when)

  The ground shook **violently**. (how)

  Then everything became quiet. (when)

  I looked **around**. (where)

  Mom said, "Come **here**, Trudy." (where)

- Adverbs add details and bring life to your writing.

  I went to find Mom. The house creaked. (without adverbs)

  I **quickly** went **upstairs** to find Mom. The house creaked **noisily**. (with adverbs)

Try It

A. Complete each sentence. Use an adverb from the box.

down	everywhere	immediately	loudly
nervously	quickly	quietly	suddenly

1. The ground rumbled _____.

2. I was scared. My heart beat _____.

3. Things started to fall _____.

4. Cracks _____ appeared in the walls.

5. Mom yelled _____ at my sister and me.

6. "Get under the table _____!" she cried.

7. We heard a crash. The ceiling fell _____.

8. We _____ waited for the shaking to stop.

B. Write an adverb to complete each sentence. Use the clues in parentheses to help you.

9. _____ the house stopped shaking. **(when)**

10. We were under the table. We stayed _____ for a while. **(where)**

11. _____, Mom crawled out. **(when)**

12. My sister stood up and looked around _____. **(how)**

13. Mom walked _____ around the room. **(how)**

14. Pieces of plaster lay on the floor _____. **(where)**

C. Complete each sentence. Write an adverb.

15. _____ I followed Mom and my sister.

16. "Look at our house," my sister said _____.

17. "Go outside _____," Mom said to us.

18. "We won't be safe _____."

19. _____, though, we found Snowball, our kitten.

20. Then we all went _____.

D. Rewrite each sentence. Add one adverb.

21. The earthquake damaged every house on our street. _____

_____

22. I looked and saw a tree on the ground. _____

_____

23. My neighbors walked over and spoke to us. _____

_____

24. Someone said, "We are lucky to be alive." _____

_____

✓Use the Correct Verb Tense

- **Past tense** verbs show an action that already happened.
- Add **-ed** to regular verbs to talk about the past.
- Use special past tense forms for irregular verbs.

Present	Past	Example in the Past
start	start**ed**	The storm **started**.
crash	crash**ed**	Thunder **crashed**.
find	found	People **found** shelter in an empty school.
bring	brought	They **brought** food into the school.

- When you write, don't change verb tense unless you want to show that things happen at a different time.

    The streets **flooded**. Families ~~leave~~ ^{left} town.

Try It

A. Complete each sentence. Write the past tense form of the verb in parentheses.

1. Last year, it _____ hard for days. **(rain)**

2. The river in our town _____. **(flood)**

3. Water _____ people's basements. **(fill)**

4. Furniture _____ in the deep water. **(float)**

5. We _____ our table in the next yard. **(find)**

B. (6–10) Edit the paragraph. Find and fix five incorrect verbs.

    Last year, floods destroyed parts of our town. Deep water covers towns and farms. Volunteers work hard for days. They pack sandbags for dams. They bringed people food and water. They help animals to safety.

> **Mark Your Changes**
>
> Replace with this.
>
> Last week, people ~~row~~ ^{rowed} boats down the street.

✔ Check Your Spelling
Words with Suffixes

When you add a suffix that begins with a vowel, drop the final **e** from a base word that ends with **e**. If the base word does not end in an **e**, then adding the suffix usually does not change the spelling of the base word.

Base Word	Suffix	New Word
take	**-ing**	**taking**
like	**-ed** or **-ing**	**liked** or **liking**
repair	**-ed** or **-ing**	**repaired** or **repairing**

Try It

A. Complete each sentence. Add the correct suffix to the word in parentheses.

1. Students are _____ about hurricanes. **(learn)**

2. One hurricane _____ over my state last year. **(pass)**

3. Strong winds _____ many homes. **(damage)**

4. Heavy rains _____ the streets. **(fill)**

5. Some houses _____ . **(collapse)**

6. Now people are _____ stronger buildings. **(make)**

B. (7–12) Edit the paragraph. Find and fix six spelling errors.

I am readed about what happend to New Orleans in 2005.
Hurricane Katrina causd many problems. The flood waters
destroyeed neighborhoods. Many people are startting to return to
New Orleans. They are hopeing to rebuild.

Mark Your Changes

Replace with this.
waded
They ~~wadeed~~ through
deep water.

✓ Check for Capital Letters

When you use a proper noun, always capitalize it.

Proper Nouns	Examples
Proper nouns include the following: • months, days, special days, and holidays • names of places	**A**pril, **T**uesday, **E**arth **D**ay **T**exas, **L**os **A**ngeles

Try It

A. **Edit each sentence. Correct capitalization errors.**

1. In 1978, there was a huge blizzard in new england.

2. The snow began one morning in february.

3. People in many Cities couldn't go to work.

4. Students in boston couldn't go to school.

5. The Snowstorm lasted for hours.

Mark Your Changes

Capitalize.

It is very cold in january.

Make lowercase.

Sometimes we ice skate on the Lake.

B. **(6–12) Edit the paragraph. Find and fix seven capitalization errors.**

I lived in massachusetts in 1978 and saw the blizzard.

The snow was over four feet deep in my town near the atlantic

Ocean! We were sent home from School on monday, February 6.

We were still out of school on valentine's day! Some people used

skis on city streets. Others walked on the frozen charles River.

Use Past Tense Verbs

Remember: Use a verb in the present tense to show that an action happens now or often. Use a verb in the past tense to show that an action happened before now.

- Add **-ed** to most verbs to form the past tense.

  Earlier today, Akiko **walked** on the mountain trail.

- If a verb ends in silent **e**, drop the **e**. Then add **-ed**.

  A sudden rainstorm **surprised** her.

- Some one-syllable verbs end in one vowel and one consonant. Double the consonant before you add **-ed**.

  Akiko **jogged** toward a hut on the trail.

- The verb **be** has special forms. **Was** is the past tense form for **am** and **is**. **Were** is the past tense form for **are**.

  The ground **was** wet. The rocks **were** slippery.

Try It

A. Write the correct verb to complete each sentence.

1. A few hours ago, Akiko _____ on a wet rock.
   slips / slipped

2. Her ankle _____ very sore after she fell.
   was / is

3. Akiko _____ her cell phone. She called for help.
   uses / used

4. Now she _____ safely in the hut.
   rests / rested

B. Complete each sentence. Write the past tense form of the verb in parentheses.

5. Akiko _____ her ankle in a bandage. **(wrap)**

6. Then she _____ for help to come. **(wait)**

7. She _____ ready for a problem like this. **(be)**

8. Of course, Akiko _____ her experience! **(survive)**

Use Irregular Past Tense Verbs

Remember: Some verbs have a special form for the past tense.

Verbs that have a special form for the past tense are called **irregular verbs**. Here are some irregular verbs.

PRESENT	PAST	PRESENT	PAST
have, has	had	meet, meets	met
do, does	did	make, makes	made
get, gets	got	say, says	said
bring, brings	brought	tell, tells	told

Try It

A. Complete each sentence. Write the correct verb.

1. Chris _____ a creative idea a few months ago.
   has / had

2. Last month, he _____ together with his friends.
   got / get

3. They _____ in the woods near Chris's house.
   meet / met

4. "I _____ a great idea," he _____ .
   have / has   said / sayed

5. Then he _____ them, "Let's build a shack in the woods."
   tells / told

B. Complete each sentence. Write the past tense form of the verb in parentheses.

6. The friends _____ supplies to the woods. **(bring)**

7. They _____ a lot of work to do. **(have)**

8. _____ they work hard? Yes, they _____ . **(do)**

9. They _____ a strong shack. **(make)**

10. Chris _____ , "Long ago, shacks like this helped people to survive." **(say)**

Use Different Types of Sentences

Remember: Use a command to tell someone what to do.

- A **statement** tells something. End the statement with a period.

  Uncle Max lives in a snowy place. He is always alert.

- An **exclamation** shows strong feeling. End the exclamation with an exclamation point.

  This is a terrible snowstorm! Uncle Max's car is stuck!

- A **command** begins with a verb. The subject (**you**) is understood. End most commands with a period.

  Be ready for an emergency. Have a survival kit.

Try It

A. Read each sentence. Add the punctuation mark that you think belongs at the end. Then write whether the sentence is a **statement**, an **exclamation**, or a **command**.

1. Uncle Max is hungry _____

2. Find some granola in the survival kit _____

3. I am really cold in this car _____

4. Get inside the sleeping bag _____

B. Put the words in the correct order to make a negative statement.

5. not / My uncle / was / afraid / .

   _____

6. thirsty or cold / not / He / was / .

   _____

7. Rescuers / take a long time / did / not / to come / .

   _____

8. did / until the next day / stop / The snow / not / .

   _____

REMEMBER
• The word **not** is an **adverb**. It can make a statement negative.
• Put **not** after all forms of **be**.
• Put **not** between **did** and an action verb.

Use Verbs in the Future Tense

- The tense, or time, of a verb shows when an action happens.

PAST	PRESENT	FUTURE
(before now)	(now)	(after now)

- Use the **future tense** to tell about something that will happen later. To form the future tense, add **will** before the main verb.

    My family **will move** soon.

    I **will go** to a new school.

    On the first day of school, I **will look** for a friend.

Try It

A. Change each sentence to the future tense. Write the new sentence.

1. I join the Young Chefs Club at school. _____

_____

2. The club meets at 3:30 p.m. on Friday. _____

_____

3. I find new friends there. _____

_____

4. The teacher shows us delicious, simple recipes. _____

_____

B. Complete each sentence. Use the future tense of the verb in parentheses.

5. The Young Chefs Club _____ our families to a special dinner. **(invite)**

6. Some students _____ spaghetti and salad. **(make)**

7. Other students _____ desserts. **(bake)**

8. Of course, everyone _____ this meal! **(love)**

73 Use Verbs in the Future Tense

- The tense, or time, of a verb shows when an action happens.

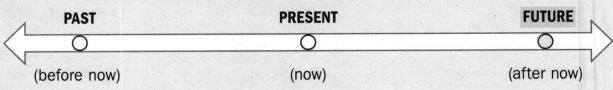

PAST	PRESENT	FUTURE
(before now)	(now)	(after now)

- Use the **future tense** to tell about something that will happen later. To form the future tense, add **will** before the main verb.

  The bell **will ring** soon. Mia **will go** into school.

- You can use a contraction to shorten a pronoun and **will**. An apostrophe (') takes the place of the letters you leave out.

She will feel shy.	**I will** help her.	**We will** do well.
She'll feel shy.	**I'll** help her.	**We'll** do well.

- You also can shorten **will** and **not**. Use the contraction **won't**.

Mia **will not** know anyone.	It **will not** take long to make friends.
Mia **won't** know anyone.	It **won't** take long to make friends.

Try It

A. Complete each sentence. Write the future tense of the verb in parentheses.

1. Mia _____ the school office first. **(visit)**

2. Then she _____ to some classes. **(go)**

3. I _____ lunch with Mia. **(eat)**

B. Make a contraction from the future tense words. Write the new sentence.

4. Mia will not go home right after school. _____

5. She will talk to the music teacher. _____

6. Then I will take her to the softball coach. _____

74 Use Verbs in the Future Tense

- The **future tense** of a verb shows that an action will happen later.

PAST	PRESENT	FUTURE
(before now)	(now)	(after now)

- You can use a form of **be** with **going to** and a **main verb** to tell about the future.

Subject	Form of Be	Example
I	am	I **am going to see** my cousin, Jun Ming.
you	are	You **are going to come** with me.
he, she, it	is	He **is going to visit** us from China.
we	are	We **are going to meet** him at my grandparents' house.
they	are	They **are going to give** us a good meal, too.

Try It

A. Read each sentence. Then write it in the future tense. Use a form of be and going to.

1. I take Jun Ming to the city. _____

2. We visit the science museum. _____

3. My mom meets us there. _____

B. Complete these sentences in the future tense. Use am, is, or are and going to.

4. Jun Ming _____ stay with me all summer.

5. We _____ have a lot of fun.

75 Ask a Question About the Future

- Use the **future tense** to tell about an action that will happen later.

  Isabel **will visit** Anita today. Anita **is going to make** lunch.

- You can ask and answer questions about the future. Use **Yes** or **No** in each answer.

Statement	Question	Answer
Anita **will make** tacos.	**Will** Anita **make** tacos?	Yes, she **will**. No, she **won't**.
Isabel **is going to bring** dessert.	**Is** Isabel **going to bring** dessert?	Yes, she **is**. No, she **isn't**.

Try It

A. Change each statement into a question. Write the question and an answer that begins with Yes or No.

1. Isabel is going to walk to Anita's house. _____

   _____

2. They are going to eat soon. _____

   _____

3. The lunch will begin an afternoon of fun. _____

   _____

B. Read each answer. Write a question for it. Use the future tense.

4. Yes, she is. _____

5. No, she won't. _____

6. Yes, they will. _____

76 Ask Questions with *How*

- Some questions ask for **Yes** or **No** answers. The answers are short.

   Will you give me baseball tips, Nate? **Yes**, I will.

   Will they be hard to learn? **No**, they won't.

- Questions that start with **How** often ask for explanations. The answers give more information.

   How will you help me? I will show you examples.

Question	Answer
How do you learn to play a sport well?	You practice every day.
How will Peter get to know Nate?	He will invite him for pizza.

Try It

A. Change each question into a **How** question. Write the question and an answer for it.

1. Does Nate help Peter? _____

_____

2. Does Peter thank Nate? _____

_____

3. Will the boys share a meal? _____

_____

B. Read each answer. Then write a **How** question for it.

4. Nate slices vegetables for the pizza. _____

5. Peter puts the sauce and cheese on top. _____

6. That pizza will taste delicious! _____

77 Ask Questions with *Why*

- Some questions ask for **Yes** or **No** answers. The answers are short.
  Will Lupe eat with us? **Yes**, she will.
  Will Vera join us? **No**, she won't.

- Questions that start with **Why** ask for reasons. The answers give more information.
  Why are we going to the restaurant? We want to eat Mexican food.

Question	Answer
Why will Lupe go to the restaurant?	She will meet her friends there.
Why does Lupe order burritos?	She likes them.

Try It

A. Change each question into a **Why** question. Write the question and an answer for it.

1. Is the restaurant busy? _____

_____

2. Will Lupe order a large meal? _____

_____

3. Do her friends eat all the nachos? _____

_____

B. Read each answer. Then write a **Why** question for it.

4. Lupe loves ice cream. _____

5. This restaurant has great food. _____

6. Lupe wants her family to try the food. _____

Name _____ Date _____

78 Use Verbs in the Present and Future Tense

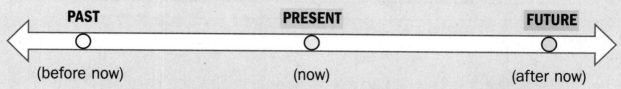

- The tense, or time, of a verb shows when an action happens.

PAST	PRESENT	FUTURE
(before now)	(now)	(after now)

- Use the **present tense** for an action that happens now or that happens often. Add **-s** to the verb when one person or thing does the action.

    Jen **makes** her own clothes. Her sisters **make** clothes, too.

- Use the **future tense** to tell about something that will happen later. To form the future tense, use **will** or a form of **be** with **going to** before the main verb.

    Jen **will help** the Drama Club. She **is going to sew** costumes.

Try It

A. Complete each sentence. Write the verb that shows the correct tense.

1. Right now, Jen _____ a costume.
   design / designs

2. Leah shares an idea. The two girls often _____ together.
   work / will work

3. Tomorrow, Jen _____ her sewing machine.
   uses / will use

4. They _____ all the costumes next week.
   finish / will finish

5. At the next practice, the actors _____ the costumes.
   wear / will wear

B. (6–10) Tell what happens. Use present tense verbs and future tense verbs to complete the paragraph.

The play _____ this evening at 7:00 p.m. Right now, though,

the actors _____ one last time. Jen _____

the actors put on their costumes now, too. All the students _____

well together at this rehearsal. Tonight, the audience _____ the

play—and the costumes!

Use Verb Tenses

PAST	PRESENT	FUTURE
(before now)	(now)	(after now)

The **tense** of a verb tells when an action happens. Use the correct form of a verb to show that the action is in **past**, **present**, or **future** time.

- Use the **past tense** for an action before now. Add **-ed** or use a special form.

  Omar **painted** his first picture last year. He **took** an art class then.

- Use the **present tense** for an action that is happening now or that happens again and again. Add **-s** to the verb when you talk about one other person or one thing.

  Omar **paints** a lot now. He **takes** more art classes.

- Use the **future tense** to show that something is going to happen later. Use **will** before the main verb.

  Omar **will paint** an important piece of art. It **will take** some hard work.

Try It

A. Write each sentence. Change the <u>verb</u> to the past tense.

1. Omar <u>will join</u> the Art Club. _____

2. He <u>helps</u> with the work on a mural. _____

3. First, the students carefully <u>measure</u> the wall. _____

   _____

4. For a whole week, they <u>design</u> the mural. _____

   _____

5. At the end of the week, the mural <u>will go</u> onto the wall by the gym. _____

   _____

B. Write the present tense verb that correctly completes each sentence.

6. Omar _____ to Art Club meetings two times a week.
   goes / went

7. Right now, the students _____ about another mural.
   talked / talk

8. Omar has an idea. He _____ a design for the mural.
   drew / draws

9. Omar _____ to paint.
   start / starts

10. He _____ the yellow paint first.
    uses / used

C. Complete each sentence. Write the future tense of a verb from the box.

fill	look	paint	show	think	want

11. Omar _____ about murals for his family.

12. Perhaps he _____ a rain forest scene for Natalie.

13. It _____ plants and colorful birds.

14. Mom _____ white clouds in a blue sky.

15. Her wall _____ very peaceful.

16. Race cars _____ a wall in Omar's room.

D. Write each sentence. Fix the mistake in the <u>verb</u>.

17. Last week, members of the Art Club <u>finish</u> another mural. _____

    _____

18. Shane <u>writed</u> about the murals for the school paper. _____

    _____

19. Right now, television reporters <u>interviews</u> the artists. _____

    _____

20. Tomorrow, the murals <u>appears</u> on the news! _____

    _____

Use Prepositions

Use **prepositions** to tell about the location of one thing compared to another. Some common prepositions are **in**, **on**, **over**, **under**, and **next to**.

The girl is **in** the library.
Her hands are **over** the keyboard.
The keys are **under** her fingers.
The boy is **next to** a bookshelf.
Many books are **on** the shelf.

Try It

A. What else might you see in a library? Write a preposition from the box to complete each sentence.

in	on	over	next to	under

1. The librarian is _____ a bookshelf.

2. The bookshelf is low. It is _____ the wall clock.

3. The new magazines are _____ the shelf.

4. Some students are _____ the library. They speak too loudly.

5. The librarian points to the "Quiet" sign. It is _____ the door.

B. Write a sentence with each preposition about things you might see in a gym.

6. on _____

7. next to _____

8. under _____

9. in _____

10. over _____

79 Use Prepositions to Show Location

Use **prepositions** to show where someone or something is.

| in | on | above over | below under | beside next to |

Phil runs **on** the track.
The track is **next to** the school.
The scoreboard is **above** the bleachers.

Try It

A. Complete each sentence with a preposition that shows location.

1. Some track events are _____ the field.

2. The high jumpers jump _____ a bar.

3. The throwing events are _____ the track.

4. People sit _____ the bleachers to watch.

5. The runners put their bags _____ the bench.

B. Complete each sentence. Choose the correct preposition.

6. The runners race _____ this track.
   on / under

7. The coach stands _____ the track.
   next to / over

8. Phil runs _____ Deon.
   under / beside

9. Each runner stays _____ his lane.
   in / above

10. At the end, Phil holds the first-place medal _____ his head.
    in / over

80 Use Prepositions to Show Direction

Use **prepositions** to show which way someone or something goes.

up   **down**   **through**   **across**   **into**

Amelia marches **down** the hall.
She goes **into** the school library.
She walks **across** the room and then sits.

Try It

A. Complete each sentence with a preposition that shows direction.

1. Amelia looks _____ her history book.

2. Her eyes go _____ the pages.

3. Then Amelia walks _____ the aisle.

4. She goes _____ the computer room.

5. She walks _____ the room to a computer.

B. Use words from each column to build sentences. Write the sentences.

Amelia	enters	down the computer screen.
Andrew	scrolls	through the door.
The librarian	sits	across the aisle from Amelia.

6. _____

7. _____

8. _____

81 Use Prepositions to Show Time

Use **prepositions** to show when something happens.

- Some prepositions show **time of day**.
    Sean's day begins **at** 6:00 **in** the morning.
    That is **in** one hour.

- Some prepositions show **days**, **months**, or **years**.
    Sean started soccer **in** September.
    His first game is **on** Friday.

Try It

A. Write in, at, or on to complete each sentence.

1. School starts _____ 7:15 a.m.

2. _____ Mondays, Sean has both band and soccer practice.

3. He leaves school _____ 6:30 p.m.

4. Sean does his homework _____ the evening.

5. This busy schedule will end _____ November.

6. Sean's last soccer game is _____ his birthday.

**B. (7–12) Write about Sean's weekend. Use in, at, or on to complete
the paragraph.**

_____ Saturday, Sean has a soccer game. That is the last Saturday

_____ November. Sean has to be there early _____ the

morning. The game starts _____ 9:00 a.m. Sean doesn't have a game

_____ Sunday. He is glad for the day off! Then hockey practice begins

_____ December.

82 Use Prepositions to Show Location

At, **on**, and **in** are **prepositions**. They can tell where something is.

- Use **at** to show **an exact location**.
  The friends are **at** their school.
  They are **at** the front entrance.

- Use **on** to show **locations on streets**.
  The school is **on** Troy Road.
  The pool is **on** Main Street.

- Use **in** to show **a bigger area**.
  The friends live **in** Plainsville.
  Is Plainsville **in** Texas?

Try It

A. Write **at**, **on**, or **in** to complete each sentence.

1. Troy met me _____ the bulletin board in the library yesterday.

2. The library is _____ Williams Avenue.

3. A poster said, "We need tutors _____ the teen center."

4. The teen center is _____ Plainfield.

5. The tutoring room is _____ the back of the building.

B. (6–12) Write **at**, **on**, or **in** to complete the paragraph.

Troy will be a math tutor _____ the teen center tomorrow. It is
_____ Taylor Road. I will also be a math tutor there. I live nearby,
_____ Redmont. We will meet _____ the train station.
The station is _____ Greene Street. Later, we will eat lunch
_____ Center City. We will eat _____ a new restaurant.

83 Use Prepositions to Show Time

You can use **prepositions** like **at**, **on**, and **in** to talk about time.

- Use **at** to tell about **an exact time**.
  The championship game begins **at** 7:00 p.m.
- Use **on** to tell about **a longer period of time**.
  The game is **on** Friday night.
- Use **in** to tell about **an even longer period of time**.
  The game is **in** March.

Try It

A. Write **at**, **on**, or **in** to complete each sentence.

1. The championship soccer game is _____ the fall.

2. It is always _____ a Saturday morning.

3. The championship basketball game, however, is _____ the winter.

4. It is always _____ a Friday night.

5. I am so excited. The game is _____ three days!

6. Let's meet _____ 6:00 p.m. on the night of the game.

B. (7–12) Write **at**, **on**, or **in** to complete the paragraph.

It's finally game night! The team comes into the gym _____ 6:30 p.m. The referees arrive _____ 6:45 p.m. This is the biggest school event _____ March. There is no better place to be _____ this Friday night. _____ halftime, our team is ahead. _____ Saturday, will we celebrate a big win?

84 Use Prepositions

Prepositions have many uses. Here are some common prepositions:

about	for	from	to	with

My friend Rosa is **from** Brazil.
She lived there **for** many years.
Rosa moved **to** the United States.
She came here **with** her family.
She tells me **about** her childhood there.

Try It

A. Complete each sentence. Use **about**, **for**, **from**, **to**, or **with**.

1. My friends come _____ different countries.

2. We all moved _____ this country.

3. I lived there _____ fifteen years.

4. I thought _____ my old home many times.

5. Now I am happy _____ my new friends.

6. We go _____ many events together.

B. (7–14) Complete the paragraph. Use prepositions from the box.

Soo moved here _____ South Korea. She went back _____ the summer. She stayed _____ her grandparents. She wrote a journal _____ her trip. She took the journal _____ her everywhere she went. Later, Soo showed it _____ me. The journal told stories _____ her trip. I read the stories _____ many hours!

Use Prepositional Phrases

- **Prepositions** show different things. Some prepositions show **location**.
  Some students are **in** this hallway.
  Others are in the hallway **above** this one.

- Some prepositions show **direction**.
  Kira often walks **through** the school alone.
  Other students go **into** their classes together.

- Some prepositions have many uses.
  Schoolwork is hard **for** me.
  My brother has an easier time **with** schoolwork.

- A **prepositional phrase** is a group of words that starts with a preposition and ends with a noun or pronoun. You can use a prepositional phrase to add details.

- Study these sentences. Notice that they are plain:
  Sometimes I walk alone.
  Sometimes Amy and I walk together.

- These sentences are more interesting:
  Sometimes I walk alone **in school**.
  Sometimes Amy and I walk **down the hall** together.

Try It

A. Write the preposition that correctly completes each sentence.

1. Different kinds of students walk _____ these hallways.
   with / through

2. Keiko often enjoys sports events _____ her friends.
   with / about

3. Austin, though, usually stays _____ home.
   into / at

4. My best friends read _____ hours.
   for / about

5. I spend a lot of time _____ the gym.
   with / in

B. Use a prepositional phrase from the box to complete each sentence.

about sports	**across the pool**	**down snowy hills**
for the newspaper	**in her room**	**with his friends**

6. Marissa is a strong swimmer. She swims many laps _____.

7. Rafi is a friendly person. He usually runs _____.

8. Sue is a quiet person. She plays computer games _____.

9. Henry loves books about soccer. He often reads _____.

10. Tamara is a writer. She works part-time _____.

11. I enjoy winter sports. I usually ski _____.

C. Write a prepositional phrase to complete each sentence. Choose prepositions from the box. (You will not use every preposition.)

about	**above**	**at**	**down**	**for**
from	**in**	**into**	**through**	**with**

12. Cassie, a girl _____, is a great artist.

13. Cassie is friends _____.

14. Another classmate is very good _____.

15. Josh likes basketball. He is never far _____.

16. Josh shoots the basketball _____.

D. Rewrite each sentence. Add a prepositional phrase to give more details.

17. Students will present a play this weekend.

_____

18. Some students write stories.

_____

Use Object Pronouns

- In English, sentences often follow the **S-V-O** pattern. There is a **subject** (**S**), a **verb** (**V**), and an **object** (**O**).

  The **principal** **announced** a **show**.
  subject   verb   object

  The **students** **liked** that **idea**.
  subject   verb   object

- Special forms of pronouns are used to replace nouns that are the objects of verbs. These are called **object pronouns**.

  Hana **hung** **posters** on the walls.
  subject verb   object

  She also **put** **them** on bulletin boards.
  subject   verb object
  pronoun   pronoun

Subject Pronoun	Object Pronoun
I	me
you	you
he	him
she	her
it	it
we	us
they	them

- Study the subject and object pronouns. Remember to use an object pronoun to replace an object noun in a sentence.

Try It

A. Read each sentence. Replace the <u>object noun</u> with an object pronoun. Write the new sentence.

1. Hana told <u>friends</u> about the show. _____

2. Ivan helped <u>Hana</u>. _____

3. Leah learned <u>a song</u>. _____

B. Write the pronoun that correctly completes each sentence.

4. Leah found Tim. She needed _____ to help.
   us / him

5. "Will you help _____ , Tim?" Leah asked.
   me / them

6. "I will help _____ , Leah," Tim said.
   us / you

85 Use Nouns as Objects

A **noun** names a person, place, or thing.

- A noun can be the **subject** of a sentence.

  Kim sings the words to the song.
  subject

- A noun can also be the **object** of an **action verb**. To find the object, turn the verb into a question: "Plays what?" The answer is the object: **song**.

  Latoya **plays** the **song** on the guitar.
  verb   object

- Many English sentences follow this pattern: subject → verb → object.

  The **girls practice** the **song** together.
  subject   verb   object

Try It

A. Complete each sentence. Use an object from the box.

Kim	music	time	words

1. Latoya practices the _____ on her guitar.

2. Kim learns the _____ to the song.

3. Latoya meets _____ in the music room.

4. They spend _____ together every day.

B. Complete each sentence. Write an object noun.

5. Mr. Green hears the girls' _____.

6. He sees the two _____ in the music room.

7. "Will you share your _____ at the talent show?" he asks.

8. "Our talent show needs good _____."

86 Use Object Pronouns

A **pronoun** refers to a noun. Some pronouns are **object pronouns**.

- Use an **object pronoun** after an **action verb**.

  Raul **takes me** to the rehearsal.

- Use an **object pronoun** after a **preposition**.

  He hands a microphone **to me**.

  Then I sing a song **with him**.

Object Pronouns	
Singular	**Plural**
me	us
you	you
him, her, it	them

Try It

A. Read each sentence. Write the object pronoun that replaces the underlined word or words.

1. Kelsey walks onto <u>the stage</u>. _____

2. She sits next to <u>Johanna</u>. _____

3. "Will you sing for <u>Mr. Green and Mrs. Chin</u>?" Mr. Green and Mrs. Chin ask. _____

4. Kelsey looks nervously at <u>the students</u>. _____

5. "Who will play the piano for <u>Kelsey</u>?" Kelsey asks. _____

B. Use an object pronoun to complete the second sentence in each pair.

6. Craig rehearses for <u>the show</u>. He will juggle in _____.

7. Nikki helps <u>Craig</u>. She hands juggling clubs to _____.

8. Craig takes <u>the clubs</u>. He juggles with _____.

9. Craig looks at <u>Nikki</u>. He gets a juggling ring from _____.

10. The students point at <u>Craig</u>. They cheer for _____.

87 Use Object Pronouns

- An **object pronoun** comes after an **action verb** or a **preposition**.

  Max gets Kelsey onto the stage. He **introduces her**.

  Max points to Kelsey. He claps **for her**.

- The object pronoun must go with the **noun** it refers to.

  Kelsey walks to the **microphone**. She stands next to **it**.

  She looks at **Zack** at the piano. She nods at **him**.

  I cheer for these **performers**. I really like **them**.

Try It

A. Write an object pronoun to complete the second sentence in each pair. Underline the noun it refers to.

1. Next, the audience sees Craig. Nikki comes onto the stage with _____.

2. Craig juggles four beanbags. He doesn't drop _____.

3. The people watch the juggling act. They love _____.

4. Then I see Kim and Latoya on stage. I smile at _____.

5. I listen to Kim. Latoya plays the piano for _____.

B. (6–10) Write object pronouns to complete the paragraph.

The talent show is over. I enjoyed all the acts. Everyone else liked

_____ , too. The performers thanked Mr. Green and Mrs. Chin.

The students also gave flowers to _____. I looked for Craig. I spoke

with _____ after the show. Craig saw Nikki. He thanked _____.

She was a great help to _____ onstage.

88 Name Yourself Last

- **Me** is an object pronoun. Use **me** after an **action verb** or after a **preposition**.

    Mrs. Chin **saw me** after the show.

    She spoke **with me** for several minutes.

- Sometimes you talk about somebody else and yourself. Use the pronoun **me** last.

    Matt helps **Julie and me** after the show.

    He cleans up with **her and me**.

Try It

A. Rewrite each sentence. Write about somebody else and yourself correctly.

1. Mrs. Reynolds has a party for the performers and I. _____

    _____

2. Kim sings a song for me and Max. _____

3. Craig juggles with I and Latoya. _____

4. The party is fun for me and my friends. _____

B. Write the words in the correct order to make a sentence.

5. Chris / goes to the party / and me / with you _____

    _____

6. sees / me / Grace and / John / at the party _____

    _____

7. Rosa sings / with / a song / me / Henry / and _____

    _____

8. the piano / and / me / Latoya plays / for / my friends _____

    _____

89 Use Gerunds as Objects

Some verbs that end in **-ing** can act like nouns. When they come after action verbs, they are **objects** of the verbs. They are called **gerunds**.

Emily Dickinson loved **writing**.

She also enjoyed **reading**. What do you enjoy?

Try It

A. Write a word from the box to complete each sentence.

calling	drawing	rolling	running	sitting	writing

1. I love _____ poems about nature.

2. Sometimes I like _____ fast along the beach.

3. I often enjoy _____ in a chair next to the water.

4. I like _____ in my sketch pad, too.

5. I usually hear the _____ of seagulls.

6. I make the _____ of the waves into poems.

B. Write the words in the correct order. Make sure that the object ends in **-ing**.

7. Mom / reading at the beach / likes _____

8. enjoys / fishing / Dad _____

9. My sister / finding / seashells / tries _____

10. in the sand / goes / digging / My dog _____

11. playing / My brother / loves / in the waves _____

_____

12. We all / like / for walks together / going _____

90 Reflexive Pronouns

Use a **reflexive pronoun** to talk about the same person or thing twice in a simple sentence. Reflexive pronouns end in -**self** or -**selves**.

I make my**self** write for an hour each day.

My **brother** takes time for him**self**, too.

People often walk by them**selves** in the park.

Reflexive Pronouns	
Singular	**Plural**
myself	ourselves
yourself	yourselves
himself, herself, itself	themselves

Try It

A. Write the reflexive pronoun that completes each sentence correctly.

1. We are reading some poems to _____.
   himself / ourselves

2. I like to read poems by _____.
   myself / ourselves

3. Ella told _____ to share her poem with her friends.
   herself / yourself

4. My friends remind _____ to thank Ella for her poem.
   itself / themselves

5. Ella, will you write a new poem by _____ or with me?
   yourself / yourselves

B. Write a reflexive pronoun to complete each sentence.

6. Will the two of you do that poetry project by _____?

7. I put _____ into each picture in the project.

8. We also promise _____ to read more poetry.

9. Angela bought a book of poems by Emily Dickinson for _____.

10. More students should buy _____ poetry books.

Use Subject and Object Pronouns

- Review the forms of subject and object pronouns.

Subject Pronoun	I	you	he	she	it	we	they
Object Pronoun	me	you	him	her	it	us	them

- Use a **subject pronoun** to replace a noun that is in the subject position in a sentence.

  Bernardo is a new student. **He** moved here this summer.

- Use an **object pronoun** to replace a noun that is used as the object of a verb.

  Marci meets Bernardo. Marci likes **him**.

- Also use an **object pronoun** after a **preposition**.

  Marci eats lunch with Bernardo. Marci learns **about him**.

Try It

A. Complete each sentence. Use a subject pronoun.

1. Bernardo likes poetry. _____ writes poems.

2. Marci does, too. _____ is a good writer.

3. "_____ am in the Writing Club," Marci says.

4. "Bernardo, _____ should come to a meeting."

5. Bernardo sees Marci after school. _____ go to the meeting.

6. _____ is a fun time for everybody.

7. "_____ all write," the members tell Bernardo.

8. Bernardo is happy. _____ has new friends.

B. Complete each sentence. Use an object pronoun.

9. Bernardo reads some poems. Club members love _____.

10. The students publish a magazine. Bernardo designs a page for _____.

11. Bernardo sees Kendra. He gives a poem to _____.

12. Kendra helps Bernardo. She writes music for _____.

13. The two friends sing their song. Club members hear _____.

14. "Your song is great!" they say. "Sing your song again for _____."

C. Write the pronoun that correctly completes each sentence.

15. Club members have a music night. _____ bring their instruments.
    They / Them

16. Marci brings her brother. She plays guitar with _____.
    he / him

17. Bernardo sings with Kendra. He holds the music for _____.
    she / her

18. Bob and I play our trumpets. _____ have a lot of fun.
    We / Us

19. Then everyone performs a song together. Some sing and some play _____
    it / them
    on instruments.

20. "This club is important to _____," says Bernardo.
    I / me

D. (21–26) Write pronouns to complete the paragraph.

All the members of the Writing Club fit in. _____ all like to
write. Some of _____ write poems. Do you remember Bernardo?
_____ is a poet. I met Kendra at the Writing Club. I am like
_____ in many ways. For example, _____ both write stories.
Maybe you can come to a meeting with Bernardo. Just ask _____!

Name _____ Date _____

✔ Check Your Prepositions

- A **preposition** comes at the beginning of a **prepositional phrase**.
- When you write, use the correct preposition to show location, time, or direction.

  I sit **next to** Ramon.
  We talk together **before** class.
  Mrs. Matsumi walks **into** the room.
  She is teaching us **about** Japanese **culture**.

Some Prepositions		
Location		
by	in	next to
Time		
after	before	during
Direction		
across	into	up
Multiple Uses		
about	at	for
from	on	with

Try It

A. Write a preposition to complete each sentence.

1. I am learning _____ other cultures.

2. My classmates come _____ many countries.

3. Sometimes we talk _____ school.

4. They share their customs _____ me.

5. Many friends speak different languages _____ home.

6. Some families sailed _____ an ocean to get here!

7. Others traveled _____ airplanes.

B. (8–12) Edit the paragraph. Fix five incorrect prepositions.

You should join our International Club! We meet at Wednesday afternoons on 3:30. We get together into the small room next to the gym. Come about friends. Teach us on your culture. You'll also make new friends!

Mark Your Changes

Replace with this.

Our family is ~~at~~ *from* China.

160   © NGSP & HB

✓ Check Your Spelling
Words with Suffixes

When adding a suffix that begins with a vowel, such as **-ed** or **-ing**, to certain words, you need to double the final consonant of the word.

Double the final consonant when:

- the word has only **one syllable** and ends in a single consonant (other than **w**, **x**, **y**, or **z**).

Word	Suffix	New Word
shop	**-ed**	shopp**ed**
pin	**-ing**	pinn**ing**

- the word has **more than one syllable** and the stress is on the final syllable.

Word	Suffix	New Word
control	**-ed**	controll**ed**
forget	**-ing**	forgett**ing**

Try It

A. Complete each sentence. Add the correct suffix to the word in parentheses.

1. Mario thinks he isn't _____ in at his new school. **(fit)**

2. Celia _____ teasing Mario about his clothes. **(admit)**

3. She _____ about it at first. **(brag)**

4. Now Celia is _____ what she did. **(regret)**

B. (5–8) Edit the paragraph. Fix four spelling errors.

Principal Leon stuned students yesterday. He baned some bullies from sports events. These students are regreting their actions. Things are begining to change for the better.

> **Mark Your Changes**
>
> Replace with this.
>
>   stopped
> She s̶t̶o̶p̶e̶d̶ teasing me.

✔ Check Your Commas

- When you write a list of more than two things, separate them with **commas**.
  My school has great teachers, clubs, and sports teams.
- Do not use a comma to separate two things.
  Alicia joined the Spanish club and the science club.

Try It

A. Edit each sentence. Add or take out commas where necessary.

1. Our school should have more plays, concerts and talent shows.

2. We need more opportunities, for actors, singers, and dancers.

3. Our talent show could be held in March, April or May.

4. Many students like to tell stories poems, and jokes.

5. We can ask Ms. Ross, and Mr. Cruz to direct the shows.

6. We can invite teachers parents, and friends.

Mark Your Changes
Add a comma.
I like math, history, and music.
Take out a comma.
I have homework for English, and science.

B. Complete each sentence below. Remember to use commas where necessary.

7. Our school needs more _____

   _____ . (List three things.)

8. Two things we should change at school are _____

   _____ .

9. Students want more opportunities to _____

   _____ . (List three things.)

10. My two favorite school activities are _____

    _____ .

Use Verbs in the Future Tense

Remember: Use a verb in the future tense to show that an action will happen later.

- To form the **future tense**, add **will** before the main verb.
  Lisa **will work** at a grocery store next summer.

- You also can use a form of **be** with **going to** and a **main verb** to tell about the future.
  My other friends **are going to find** jobs, too.

- Use the correct form of a verb to show that the action is in past, present, or future time.
  Last summer, Reggie **helped** his dad at the farm stand.
  Right now, Reggie **plows** the fields.
  Next summer, Reggie **will go** to a circus camp.
  He **is going to learn** from clowns!

Try It

A. **Complete each sentence. Write the verb that shows the correct tense.**

1. Clown camp _____ next week.
   started / will start

2. Reggie's parents _____ Reggie there next Saturday.
   are going to drive / drive

3. Reggie _____ at camp for the coming month.
   stayed / will stay

4. _____ fun when he gets to camp?
   Did he have / Is he going to have

B. **Complete each sentence. Use the correct tense of the verb in parentheses.**

5. Reggie _____ for camp yesterday. **(pack)**

6. Right now he _____ at his cabin. **(arrive)**

7. Tomorrow the clown teachers _____ Reggie how to ride a unicycle. **(show)**

8. Reggie will be happy about that. He _____ this camp. **(enjoy)**

Use Prepositions

Remember: Use prepositions to show location and direction.

- **Prepositions** can show location, or where someone or something is. Some common prepositions are: **in**, **on**, **above**, **over**, **below**, **under**, **beside**, **next to**.

    Rita stays **on** the school grounds this afternoon.

    She is **in** Room 203 for a Green Group meeting.

- Prepositions can also show direction, or which way someone or something goes. Some common prepositions are: **up**, **down**, **through**, **across**, **into**.

    Ms. Martin looks **into** the room.

    Then she walks **through** the doorway.

Try It

A. Complete each sentence. Choose the correct preposition.

1. The Green Group started a recycling program _____ our school.
    in / down

2. The students put recycling bins _____ each room.
    across / into

3. The Green Group put a label _____ each bin: "FOR SCRAP PAPER."
    on / down

4. Every Friday, the Green Group walks _____ the school.
    over / through

5. Club members collect the paper. Ms. Martin drives it _____ town to the
    across / under
    recycling center.

B. Complete each sentence with a preposition.

6. There is a wooded area _____ the school.

7. Ms. Martin sees garbage _____ the woods.

8. The Green Group members walk _____ the trails.

9. They put the garbage _____ bags.

10. The students feel good when the ground _____ the trails is clean again.

Use Subject and Object Pronouns

Remember: A pronoun refers to a noun. Some pronouns are subject pronouns. Some pronouns are object pronouns.

Subject Pronoun	I	you	he	she	it	we	they
Object Pronoun	me	you	him	her	it	us	them

- Use a **subject pronoun** as the subject of a sentence.
  Luis can sing and dance. **He** is in the school musical.
- Use an **object pronoun** as the object of an **action verb**.
  Mrs. Cruz helps Luis. Mrs. Silver **helps him**, too.
- Use an **object pronoun** after a **preposition**.
  Luis practices with Sara. He dances **with her**.

Try It

A. **Write the pronoun that correctly completes each sentence.**

1. Mills High School has a musical each year. The Drama Club students perform
    in _____.
    it / him

2. This year, the students will present <u>Peter Pan</u>. _____ practice every day.
    They / Them

3. Wendy meets the Lost Boys. She becomes friends with _____.
    they / them

4. <u>Peter Pan</u> has songs about fitting in. _____ love the songs.
    I / Me

B. **Use the correct pronoun to complete the second sentence in each pair.**

5. Many students work on the musical. The actors sing and dance in _____.

6. David is a musician. _____ plays in the orchestra.

7. Nicole and Marc run the lighting. _____ have a very important job.

8. I work with Carmen and Latisha. You may help _____ make costumes.

165

Use Different Kinds of Sentences

There are four kinds of sentences. Each kind of sentence has a different purpose. Use the end mark that fits the purpose. Start every sentence with a capital letter.

Kind of Sentence	Example
• **Statement** Make a statement to tell something. End with a period.	We are going to the mountain. We will climb to the top.
• **Question** Ask a question to find out something. End with a question mark.	When are you going? How will you get there?
• **Command** Give a command to tell someone what to do. End with a period.	Drive to Littleton. Take a left at the light.
• **Exclamation** Use an exclamation to express a strong feeling. End with an exclamation point.	The view from the top is beautiful! This is the best view in the world!

Try It

A. Read each sentence. Add the punctuation mark. Then write what kind of sentence it is.

1. Do you want to climb the mountain with us _____

2. Pack a lunch _____

3. We will leave at 7:30 in the morning _____

B. Write each sentence correctly. Use correct punctuation and capitalization.

4. are we almost at the top _____

5. we finally made it _____

91 Use Complete Sentences

- A sentence expresses a complete thought. It has a **subject** and a **predicate**.

    subject | predicate
    Three friends write a play for English class.

    subject | predicate
    They make a rough draft first.

- The most important word in the subject is the **noun** or **pronoun**. The most important word in the predicate is the **verb**.

    The **students meet** after school.
    They work in the library.

Try It

A. Read each sentence. Write whether the underlined part is the subject or the predicate. Then write the most important word in it.

1. The students <u>think about ideas for their play.</u> _____

2. <u>One girl</u> lists all the ideas. _____

3. <u>The group</u> votes on their favorite idea. _____

4. The students <u>move to the computer.</u> _____

5. They <u>talk about the script.</u> _____

B. Match each subject to a predicate.

6. The three friends   read it to the class.

7. They   finish the play.

8. The students in the class   performs the play for the school.

9. The teacher   wants them to perform it.

10. The class   love the play.

92 Use Complete Sentences

- A sentence has a **subject** and a **predicate**. The most important word in the subject is the **noun** or **pronoun**. The most important word in the predicate is the **verb**.

  The **town** **is** near the mountains.

  We **learn** about my town in school.

- Some sentences begin with **There is**, **There are**, **There was**, or **There were**. Then the subject comes after the verb.

  There **is** a long **history** to my town.

  There **are** many interesting **stories** about it.

  There **was** a big **factory** here a long time ago.

  There **were** many **jobs** at the factory.

Try It

A. Rewrite each sentence. Start the sentence with **There is**, **There are**, **There was**, or **There were**.

1. No apartment buildings were in my town. _____

_____

2. A big factory was in town. _____

_____

3. Apartments are in the old factory building now. _____

_____

B. Write **There is**, **There are**, **There was**, or **There were** to complete each sentence.

4. _____ many changes in my town today.

5. _____ no train station in my town before.

6. _____ a big train station now so people can go to the city for work.

93 What Is a Fragment?

A **fragment** is a group of words that begins with a capital letter and ends with a period. It looks like a sentence, but it is not complete. A subject or a verb may be missing.

Fragments	Sentences
Is a good student.	Yuri is a good student.
Works hard in school.	He works hard in school.
Yuri's favorite subject science.	Yuri's favorite subject is science.
He English, too.	He likes English, too.

Try It

A. Read each group of words. Write whether it is a fragment or a sentence. If it is a fragment, add a subject or a verb and write the sentence.

1. Yuri a big test in science. _____

2. The test is the final exam. _____

3. Prepares hard for the test. _____

4. He all the material. _____

B. Underline the fragment in each pair of sentences. Then add a subject or a verb. Write the new sentence.

5. Some students need help. They a study group. _____

6. The students Yuri for help. He goes to the study group. _____

_____

7. Study together. They quiz each other about science. _____

8. Yuri takes the test. He an A on it! _____

94 Add a Subject to Fix a Fragment

- A complete sentence has a **subject** and a **predicate**.
- To check for a subject, ask yourself this question: Whom or what is the sentence about?

Fragments	Sentences
Volunteered in town.	**The students** volunteered in town.
Cleaned up the park.	**They** cleaned up the park.
Planted flowers.	**Marta** planted flowers.
Raked the grass.	**I** raked the grass.

Try It

A. (1–6) Find six fragments. Add a subject to fix each fragment.

Yesterday the environmental club at school had a clean-up day.

Worked at the park. Had a lot of trash in it. Picked up the trash.

Allen worked on the hiking trails. Weeded the trails. Looked great

after that. Made our town a better place.

Mark Your Changes

Add.
   The park
   ∧ is clean.

Make lowercase.
   Let's H̸ike at the park.

B. Add a subject to fix each fragment. Write the sentence.

7. Needed help at the library. _____

8. Were in boxes. _____

9. Placed books on the shelves. _____

10. Thanked him. _____

11. Visited the library. _____

12. Took books from the shelves. _____

95 Add a Predicate to Fix a Fragment

- When you write a sentence, be sure to include a **verb** in the **predicate**. If you leave the verb out, the words you write are a **fragment**.

- To check for a verb, ask yourself this question: What is happening in this sentence?

Fragments	Sentences
The play tonight.	The play **is** tonight.
Dave his friends.	Dave **calls** his friends.
His friends at Dave's house.	His friends **meet** at Dave's house.
They no money.	They **have** no money.

Try It

A. (1–6) Find six fragments. Add a verb to fix each fragment.

The friends can't go to the play. They sad at first.

Then they an idea. They can read the play instead. The

boys the script for the play. Each boy chooses a part.

The boys their parts aloud. They them out, too. The boys

are creative. They a lot of fun.

> **Mark Your Changes**
>
> Add.
>   is
> The play funny.
>   ^

B. Add a verb to fix each fragment. Write the sentence.

7. Dave's friends a snack. _____

8. They some popcorn. _____

9. Dave a good movie. _____

10. The boys the movie. _____

96 Fix a Fragment

When you write a sentence, be sure to include a **subject** and a **verb**. If you leave the subject or the verb out, the words you write are a fragment.

Fragments	Sentences
Tells me about her home.	**Grandma** tells me about her home.
Moved here last year.	**She** moved here last year.
Grandma lonely at first.	Grandma **felt** lonely at first.
She many friends now.	She **has** many friends now.

Try It

A. (1–6) Find six fragments. Add a subject or a verb to fix each fragment.

Grandma lived in her own house in the country.

Sold her house last year. Grandma to an apartment in

the city. City life different from country life. Grandma

wanted to meet friends. She the theater. Joined a theater

group. Now she in neighborhood plays.

Mark Your Changes

Add.
Grandma
∧ lives in the city.

Make lowercase.

I like to visit H̶er.

B. Add a subject or a verb to fix each fragment. Write the sentence.

7. Grandma in a play tonight. _____

8. Goes to the play. _____

9. Is a great actress. _____

10. The play wonderful. _____

Use Complete Sentences

- A complete sentence has a subject and a predicate.
- The subject always has a **noun** or a **pronoun**.
- The predicate always has one or more **verbs**.

Subject	Predicate
My **grandmother**	**lives** with us.
I	**learn** about baseball from her.
Baseball	**is** her favorite sport.

- A sentence fragment is a group of words that does not have a subject or a predicate. This fragment is missing a subject:

    Played baseball with me yesterday.

    This fragment is missing a verb:

    Grandma baseball with me yesterday.

- A complete sentence has a **subject** and a **predicate**.
    Grandma played baseball with me yesterday.

Try It

A. Choose subjects and predicates to make complete sentences. Write the sentences.

Subject	Predicate
Marcy's grandmother	plays every Wednesday.
Her team	is on a softball team.
Marcy's family	watches all of her games.

1. _____

2. _____

3. _____

B. Write a subject to complete each sentence about a family that likes softball.

4. _____ played softball in high school.

5. _____ played softball in high school, too.

6. _____ are great softball players.

7. _____ am lucky.

8. _____ is my favorite sport.

9. _____ play together all the time!

C. Write a verb to complete each sentence about a grandmother who likes theater.

10. Marcy's grandmother _____ theater.

11. She _____ Marcy to plays.

12. The two of them _____ lunch near the theater.

13. Then they _____ to the play.

14. Marcy's grandmother _____ in plays sometimes, too.

15. Once Marcy _____ in a play with her grandmother.

16. Her grandmother _____ a big part in the play.

D. Write whether each group of words is a fragment or a complete sentence. If it is a fragment, add a subject or a predicate. Write the complete sentence.

17. Marcy made her favorite dinner with her grandmother. _____

18. Marcy's favorite dinner. _____

19. Boiled the noodles in a pot. _____

20. Her grandmother. _____

21. The lasagna dinner tasted delicious. _____

22. Loved the lasagna. _____

Use Phrases and Clauses

- A **phrase** is a group of words that work together. A sentence may have several phrases.

  A good **friend** / from my school / **visited** / last Monday.

  noun phrase   prepositional phrase   verb   adverb phrase

  This sentence is complete because it has a **subject** and a **verb**. A phrase never has both, so it does not express a complete thought.

- A **clause** contains both a subject and a verb. A clause can stand alone as a sentence.

  She wore a beautiful new jacket.
  The **jacket had** silver buttons.

Try It

A. **Underline a phrase in each sentence.**

1. We hung the jacket in the hall closet.

2. Then we did homework for the whole afternoon.

3. My good friend went home.

4. She forgot her beautiful jacket!

B. **Decide whether each group of words is a phrase or a clause. If it is a phrase, use it in a sentence.**

5. I noticed the jacket later. _____

6. The beautiful new jacket. _____

_____

7. In the evening. _____

8. I did the right thing. _____

97 Use Phrases and Clauses

- A **phrase** is a group of words that work together. A sentence may have several phrases.

  A smart **girl** / in my class / **works** / at a store.

  noun phrase   prepositional phrase   verb   prepositional phrase

  This sentence is complete because it has a **subject** and a **verb**. A phrase never has both, so it does not express a complete thought.

- A **clause** contains both a subject and a verb. A clause can stand alone as a sentence.

  The **girl sells** books and CDs.

  She helps customers every day after school.

Try It

A. Underline the phrase in each sentence. Then rewrite the sentence using a different phrase.

1. Osami is my good friend. _____

2. She works in Mrs. Soga's store. _____

3. Everyone at the store likes Osami. _____

4. She is an honest person. _____

B. Rewrite each sentence below. Add the phrase in parentheses.

5. Friday, Osami found a wallet. **(at the store)** _____

_____

6. Someone left it. **(on the counter)** _____

7. The wallet was full. **(of money)** _____

8. Osami returned the wallet. **(to its owner)** _____

_____

⊛98 Use Compound Sentences

- A clause contains both a **subject** and a **verb**. An **independent clause** can stand alone as a sentence.

  Students wear different kinds of clothes.

- A **simple sentence** has only one independent clause.

  Our **school has** a dress code.

- The words **and**, **but**, and **or** are <u>**conjunctions**</u>. They join two independent clauses to form a **compound sentence**.

  Parents like the dress code, / **and** / **students obey** it.

      independent clause   conjunction   independent clause

Try It

A. **Read each sentence. Then write simple or compound to name the kind of sentence.**

1. The new dress code for our school is not complicated. _____

2. I read all the rules carefully last night with my parents. _____

3. We can choose our own clothes, or we can buy a uniform. _____

4. Students like jeans, but we may not wear them. _____

B. **Underline the two independent clauses in each compound sentence. Circle the conjunction.**

5. The teachers talked together, and they listed the rules.

6. Sneakers are acceptable, but flip-flops are not allowed.

7. Boys can wear T-shirts with sleeves, or they can wear shirts with buttons.

8. Nora has a new short skirt, but she cannot wear it to school.

99 Use Compound Sentences with *And*

- Join two clauses with a **conjunction** to form a **compound sentence**.
- You can use the conjunction **and** to join two **independent clauses** with similar ideas. A comma (**,**) comes before the conjunction.

We planned a family party.

Everyone had a job.

We planned a family party , and everyone had a job.

Try It

A. Join each pair of sentences. Use the conjunction and to form a compound sentence.

1. Cousin Mona mowed the lawn. My mom planted flowers. _____

_____

2. Uncle Saul arranged the tables. His son brought extra chairs. _____

_____

3. My brother played the guitar. My sister sang favorite songs. _____

_____

4. I promised to make sandwiches. Aunt Ida agreed to help. _____

_____

B. These compound sentences are missing the conjunction and. Fix the mistakes.

5. I sliced the meat Aunt Ida washed the lettuce. _____

_____

6. We made lots of sandwiches Auntie stacked them on a plate. _____

_____

7. I forgot to bring the sandwiches my cousins were unhappy. _____

_____

8. It was my mistake I apologized. _____

100 Use Compound Sentences with *But*

- Join two clauses with a **conjunction** to form a **compound sentence**.
- You can use the conjunction **but** to join two **independent clauses** with different or contrasting ideas. A comma (**,**) comes before the conjunction.

All my friends are great.

They are all different.

All my friends are great,

but they are all different.

Try It

A. Join each pair of sentences. Use the conjunction but to form a compound sentence.

1. Evan is in my class. He doesn't have many friends. _____

_____

2. He is really nice. Not many people know him. _____

_____

3. Evan may be quiet. He is a lot of fun. _____

_____

4. Sometimes people laugh at him. I never do. _____

_____

B. These compound sentences are missing the conjunction but. Fix the mistakes.

5. Most boys in my class like sports Evan prefers to read. _____

_____

6. People judge him by his clothes I know that isn't important. _____

_____

7. Some students don't tell the truth Evan is always honest. _____

_____

8. We all know what really matters sometimes people forget. _____

_____

101 Use Compound Sentences with *Or*

- Join two clauses with a **conjunction** to form a **compound sentence**.
- You can use the conjunction **or** to join two **independent clauses** that show a choice. A comma (**,**) comes before the conjunction.

Do you work hard at school?	**Do you work hard at school,**
Do you waste time?	**or do you waste time?**

Try It

A. Join each pair of sentences. Use the conjunction or to form a compound sentence.

1. Do you finish homework on time? Do you hand it in late? _____

_____

2. Do you study every day? Do your books stay in your locker? _____

_____

3. Will you do your homework now? Will you play video games? _____

_____

4. You can be lazy. You can choose to succeed. _____

_____

B. These compound sentences are missing the conjunction or. Fix the mistakes.

5. Can you remember all your assignments do you write them in a notebook? _____

_____

6. You should keep your handwriting neat you should type on a computer. _____

_____

7. You can study with a friend your parents can help. _____

_____

8. Should you watch TV tonight should you study instead? _____

_____

102 Combine Sentences

You can make writing sound smoother by combining two short, choppy sentences into one longer **compound sentence**. Use a comma (**,**) and a **conjunction**.

- Use **and** to join similar ideas.

  | Tino writes poetry. | **Tino writes poetry,** |
  | He uses beautiful language. | **and he uses beautiful language.** |

- Use **but** to join different or contrasting ideas.

  | The poems are great. | **The poems are great,** |
  | Tino is too shy to read them. | **but Tino is too shy to read them.** |

- Use **or** to show a choice.

  | His poems may tell a story. | **His poems may tell a story,** |
  | They may explain his feelings. | **or they may explain his feelings.** |

Try It

A. Join each pair of sentences. Use and, but, or or to form a compound sentence.

1. Tino is my neighbor. We go to school together every day. _____

_____

2. My favorite subject is science. Tino likes poetry better. _____

_____

B. (3–5) Edit the paragraph. Combine three pairs of sentences with and, but, and or.

   Tino's poems are great. He doesn't always think so. He might read one to the class. Another student might read for him. We clap for Tino. Everyone encourages him to write more.

_____

_____

_____

Combine Sentences

You can put two short sentences together to make a **compound sentence**. Use a comma and the word **and**, **but**, or **or** to join the sentences.

- Use **and** to join similar ideas.

    Juan understands math. He explains it clearly.
    Juan understands math, **and** he explains it clearly.

- Use **but** to join different or contrasting ideas.

    I like algebra. It is difficult for me.
    I like algebra, **but** it is difficult for me.

- Use **or** to show a choice.

    A math exam can be hard. It can be easy.
    A math exam can be hard, **or** it can be easy.

Try It

A. Draw a line from one clause to another to make a longer compound sentence.

1. Juan is my best friend,	but Juan is really good at it.
2. We do homework after school,	or come see me for help."
3. I explain things to Juan,	and we help each other.
4. I have trouble with math,	and she teaches us a lot.
5. Juan helps me with algebra,	but that won't help me learn math!
6. Ms. Lam is our teacher,	or we do it in the evening.
7. She says, "Do your own work,	but he doesn't tell me the answers.
8. I could copy Juan's paper,	and he explains things to me.

B. Choose the correct word in parentheses to combine each pair of sentences. Write the compound sentence.

9. We had an algebra test today. I studied for a week. **(and, but)** _____

_____

10. I worried about the test. I did very well. **(or, but)** _____

_____

11. Do you wonder how I did it? Do you already know? **(and, or)** _____

_____

C. Combine each pair of sentences with **and**, **but**, or **or**. Write the compound sentence.

12. I solved the problems carefully. I checked each answer. _____

_____

13. Sometimes I got frustrated. I didn't give up. _____

_____

14. Should I peek at Juan's test? Should I trust my own work? _____

_____

15. I decided not to look. I am proud of myself! _____

_____

D. (16–20) Rewrite the paragraph. Combine five pairs of sentences with **and**, **but**, or **or**.

Juan is great at math. I am better at writing. He has a report due next week. I am helping him. Juan can write about a president. He can write about a senator. We find information in books. Juan takes notes in his own words. He could copy sentences from a book. That would be cheating.

_____

_____

_____

_____

_____

Use Complex Sentences

- A **clause** has a **subject** and a **verb**.
- An **independent clause** can stand alone as a sentence.

  <u>**John gave** me a photo.</u>
  independent clause

- A **dependent clause** also has a **subject** and a **verb**, but it cannot stand alone as a sentence. It begins with a **conjunction**. **Because**, **since**, **when**, **before**, and **after** are conjunctions.

  before he left for college
  dependent clause

- You can use a conjunction to join a dependent clause to an independent clause. The new sentence is called a **complex sentence** and is complete.

  <u>**John gave** me a photo **before he left** for college.</u>
  independent clause   dependent clause

Try It

A. Make a complex sentence. Draw a line from each independent clause on the left to a dependent clause on the right.

1. I put the picture next to my bed   **a.** after John left.

2. I sometimes get lonely   **b.** when I feel sad.

3. The photo cheers me   **c.** since my brother is away.

B. Match each independent clause on the left with a dependent clause on the right. Write the complex sentence.

| I laugh | after I look at that photo. |
| I always feel better | because I am on John's shoulders. |

4. _____

5. _____

(103) Use Complex Sentences

- A clause has a **subject** and a **verb**.
- An **independent clause** can stand alone as a sentence.

    Carla feels happy.
    independent clause

- A **dependent clause** also has a **subject** and a **verb**. It cannot stand alone because it begins with a **conjunction**.

    because she loves her family
    dependent clause

- You can use a conjunction to join the dependent clause to an independent clause. The new sentence is called a **complex sentence** and is complete.

    Carla feels happy **because she loves** her family.
    independent clause   dependent clause

Try It

A. Make a complex sentence. Draw a line from an independent clause on the left to a dependent clause on the right.

1. Carla enjoys her brothers and sisters   **a.** before they sit down to eat.

2. They eat dinner together   **b.** when everyone is home.

3. Everyone helps get dinner ready   **c.** because they are fun.

4. They play games   **d.** after they wash the dishes.

B. Write two complex sentences about your family.

5. _____

_____

6. _____

_____

(104) Use Complex Sentences with *Because*

- A **complex sentence** has one independent clause and one dependent clause.

  Sean loves Grandpa because Grandpa had courage.
  <u>independent clause</u>   <u>dependent clause</u>

- A dependent clause begins with a **subordinating conjunction** . The subordinating conjunction **because** tells why.

  Grandpa left his country **because** he wanted a new life.

  Sean has opportunities **because** Grandpa moved.

Try It

A. Make a complex sentence. Draw a line from an independent clause to a dependent clause.

1. Grandpa left Ireland

2. He came to the United States

3. He worked hard at his job

4. We all love Grandpa very much

a. because he wanted to save money.

b. because he wanted a better life.

c. because he has done so much for us.

d. because life was so hard there.

B. Use the conjunction because to combine each pair of sentences. Punctuate your sentences correctly.

5. I want to help our family. Grandpa worked so hard. _____

   _____

6. I can help my family now. I can do jobs around the house. _____

   _____

7. I can fix things. I am good with my hands. _____

   _____

8. I want to become a carpenter. I enjoy building things. _____

   _____

105 Use Complex Sentences with *Since*

- A **complex sentence** has one independent clause and one dependent clause.

  <u>I will buy my mother a gift</u> <u>since tomorrow is her birthday.</u>
       independent clause   **dependent clause**

- A dependent clause begins with a **subordinating conjunction**. The subordinating conjunction **since** tells why.

  I bought a plant for my mother **since** she loves to garden.

  I gave my mother a daisy plant **since** that is her favorite.

Try It

A. **Make a complex sentence. Draw a line from an independent clause to a dependent clause.**

1. Mom wears gardening gloves

2. I will buy her new gloves

3. Mom's knees sometimes hurt

4. I will buy her a pair of knee pads

    a. since she has to kneel in her garden.

    b. since they will protect her knees.

    c. since her old gloves are worn out.

    d. since she wants to protect her hands.

B. **Use the conjunction *since* to combine each pair of sentences. Punctuate your sentences correctly.**

5. My brother wants to buy a present. He loves Mom, too. _____

_____

6. I tell him about gardening. He needs some ideas. _____

_____

7. He decides to buy tools. Mom can use some new ones. _____

_____

8. He decides on a special shovel. It makes gardening easier. _____

_____

106 Use Complex Sentences with *When*

The **subordinating conjunction** **when** tells when an action happens. Use **when** if the actions in the independent and dependent clauses happen at the same time.

My friends are there **when** I need them.

They help me **when** things go wrong.

Try It

A. **Make a complex sentence. Draw a line from an independent clause to a dependent clause.**

1. Jenny's kindness helps me

2. Jenny came to see me

3. She gave me a hug

4. I felt better right away

a. when I feel sad.

b. when she saw my sad face.

c. when Jenny hugged me.

d. when I didn't make the varsity basketball team.

B. **Use the words to make complex sentences. Punctuate your sentences correctly.**

5. she needs a friend / when / I try to help Jenny / . _____

_____

6. I sent her / when / a card / she got sick / . _____

_____

7. she missed school / to her / when / I brought our homework assignments / . _____

_____

8. She gave me / she felt better / a special gift / when / . _____

_____

107 Use Complex Sentences with *Before*

The **subordinating conjunction** before tells when an action happens.
Use **before** if the dependent clause tells what happens later.
I played the drums **before** I learned to play the flute.
I played the flute badly **before** I met Karin.

Try It

A. **Make a complex sentence. Draw a line from an independent clause to a dependent clause.**

1. I did not enjoy the flute

2. The sounds from my flute were awful

3. The songs were boring

4. I couldn't play fast enough

a. before Karin gave me interesting music.

b. before I learned to blow correctly.

c. before Karin became my teacher.

d. before I learned how to place my fingers.

B. **Use the conjunction before to combine each pair of sentences. Punctuate your sentences correctly.**

5. I was discouraged. Karin helped me. _____

_____

6. I did not practice much. Karin encouraged me. _____

_____

7. I found flute practice dull. I had interesting music to play. _____

_____

8. Now I practice every day. I go to school. _____

_____

108 Use Complex Sentences with *After*

The **subordinating conjunction** after tells when an action happens.
Use **after** if the dependent clause tells what happens first.

I visited my grandmother **after** school ended in June.

She asked me to help **after** we talked for a while.

Try It

A. Make a complex sentence. Draw a line from an independent clause to a dependent clause.

1. Grandma continued to live in the same apartment

a. after we decided what to give away.

2. Her children left many of their belongings with her

b. after her children grew up.

3. Grandma wanted to give away many things

c. after they moved out.

4. I placed things in bags

d. after we sorted through them.

B. Use the words to make complex sentences. Punctuate your sentences correctly.

5. we filled them with clothes / I took storage bags to a shelter / after / . _____

_____

6. We gave books / we sorted them / after / to a library / . _____

_____

7. we removed the clothes, books, and toys / after / Grandma's closets looked empty / .

_____

_____

8. she had more room in her apartment / after / Grandma was happy / . _____

_____

Combine Clauses

You can join a dependent clause to an independent clause to form a complex sentence. The clauses are joined by a conjunction. Different conjunctions have different meanings.

Conjunction	Meaning	Example
because **since**	tells why	People sometimes give gifts **because** they want to show love. Gifts are interesting **since** people often choose them carefully.
after **before**	tells the order of events	People sometimes give gifts **after** a special event. Some people look for a long time **before** they find the perfect gift.
when	tells when	A gift is perfect **when** the receiver loves it.

Try It

A. Write after or because to complete each complex sentence.

1. My mom gave me a CD _____ I finished my exams.

2. She gave it to me _____ I worked hard all year.

3. I love the songs on it _____ each one has a great melody.

4. I always feel happy and inspired _____ I listen to those songs.

5. One song became even more special to me _____ my mom told me a story about it.

B. Complete each sentence. Choose a conjunction from the box.

after	because	before	since	when

6. My mom especially loves one song on the CD _____ it brings back memories.

7. She learned the song _____ she was a camp counselor.

8. All the campers sang it _____ they went to bed at night.

9. It calmed everyone down _____ it has a beautiful melody.

10. My mother remembered many camp stories _____ she heard that song again.

C. Write a conjunction to complete each sentence.

11. I decided to sing the song at a concert _____ it is special for my mom.

12. I practiced a lot _____ I sang it for the crowd.

13. The song was a good choice _____ it was also special to other people in the audience.

14. I felt very happy _____ some people told me their stories about the song.

15. One man learned the song _____ he was a camper at my mother's camp. He was happy to hear it again!

D. Use the conjunction in parentheses. Complete each complex sentence.

16. Now the song gives me courage **(when)** _____

17. I listen to it **(before)** _____

18. The song is important to me **(because)** _____

19. My mom and I sometimes sing the song together **(since)** _____

20. I always find new meaning in it **(after)** _____

✔ Check Your Sentences

Make sure that each sentence you write is complete with a subject and a predicate. Fix any **fragments** you find.

- You may need to add a subject that tells whom or what the sentence is about.

  Paul
  Did poorly on a test last week.

- You may need to add a verb to complete the predicate.

  was
  He afraid to tell his parents.

- You may need to add both a subject and a verb.

  Paul was
  Not honest with them.

Try It

A. **Add words to fix each fragment. Write the new sentence.**

1. Paul's parents the test paper. _____

2. They Paul about his grade. _____

3. Blamed the teacher at first. _____

4. Responsible for his own bad grade. _____

5. Did not study for this important test. _____

B. **(6–10) Edit the paragraph. Find and fix five fragments. Add words to make complete sentences.**

Paul's parents talked to him about what happened. Paul

an important lesson. Needed to be honest with his parents.

His family loved him and wanted to help. Decided to study harder

next time. The right thing to do. Paul much better on the next test.

Mark Your Changes

Add these words.
It was
∧A difficult test.

Make lowercase.
It was A̸ difficult test.

Check Your Spelling
Words That Sound Alike

Homonyms are words that sound alike but have different meanings and spellings. Here are some common homonyms that are often confused with each other.

Homonym and Its Meaning	Example Sentence
to (preposition) = toward	I had never been **to** Aunt Zoe's apartment.
two (adjective) = the number 2	We rode on **two** trains.
too (adverb) = also, more than enough	My brothers came, **too**.
your (adjective) = belonging to you	"**Your** aunt will be so happy!" Mom said.
you're (contraction) = you are	"**You're** going to have fun!"

Try It

A. Complete each sentence. Use the correct homonym.

1. We got _____ Aunt Zoe's door.
   to / two / too

2. "_____ finally here!" she said.
   Your / You're

3. She gave me a hug and a kiss, _____.
   to / two / too

4. "How was _____ trip?" Aunt Zoe asked.
   your / you're

5. "We stopped _____ times," I told her.
   to / two / too

B. (6–10) Edit the paragraph. Find and fix five spelling errors.

> Later Aunt Zoe went too her piano. "What are you're favorite songs?" she asked. I named too tunes that everyone knew. "Your going to sing along!" Aunt Zoe said. She sang, to. I didn't know Aunt Zoe was such a talented musician.

Mark Your Changes

Replace with this.

too
Aunt Zoe plays the flute, to.

Check Your Commas

> The words **and**, **but**, and **or** are conjunctions. They join the clauses in a compound sentence. A comma (**,**) comes before the conjunction.
>
> | Use a Comma | Examples |
> |---|---|
> | • Before **and**, **but**, and **or** | My grandpa is interesting**,** and I want to learn more about him. |

Try It

A. Edit each sentence. Correct the punctuation errors.

> **Mark Your Changes**
>
> Add a comma.
>
> Grandpa told stories,and
> I asked him questions.

1. Grandpa likes to travel and he has been to many places.

2. Did he like Asia best or did he prefer Africa?

3. He speaks Spanish well and he can read Italian.

4. Grandpa wants to learn Chinese but he can't find a teacher.

B. Read the sentence pairs. Make each pair into one sentence. Write the new sentence. Use the correct punctuation.

5. Grandpa took me to his office. I learned about his job. _____

    _____

6. I knew he worked for a newspaper. I didn't know anything about his job. _____

    _____

7. Grandpa showed me the newsroom. We met other writers. _____

    _____

8. Could I help write a story? Would I just have to watch? _____

    _____

Use Complete Sentences

Remember: A complete sentence has a **subject** and a **predicate**.

- The most important word in the **subject** is the **noun** or **pronoun** . The most important word in the **predicate** is the **verb**.

subject   predicate

My older **brother** **works** hard at school.

subject   predicate

He **will go** to college after high school.

- A **fragment** is a group of words that looks like a sentence but is not complete. A subject or a verb may be missing.

Fragments	Sentences
1. Does his homework every night.	**Ross** does his homework every night.
2. He for all his tests.	He **studies** for all his tests.

Try It

A. Underline each fragment below. Then add a subject or a verb. Write the new sentence.

1. Ross a dream. He will be a doctor someday. _____

2. Ross volunteers at the hospital. He to some patients. _____

3. Works carefully. He wants to do a good job. _____

4. Ross likes the work. Teaches him about patient care. _____

B. (5–8) Rewrite the paragraph. Add a subject or a verb to fix four fragments.

    A few years ago, Ross was very sick. The doctor good care of him. Got better. Ross decided to become a doctor. Now Ross biology. Learns about the human body.

_____

_____

_____

Use Compound Sentences

Remember: You can make writing sound smoother by combining two short, choppy sentences into one longer compound sentence.

- A clause contains both a **subject** and a **verb**. An **independent clause** can stand alone as a sentence.

    Grandpa helps me.   **I help** Grandpa.

- You can use a comma (**,**) and a **conjunction** to join two independent clauses to form a **compound sentence**.

    Grandpa helps me, / **and** / **I help** Grandpa.

    independent clause   conjunction independent clause

- Use **and** to join similar ideas. Use **but** to join different or contrasting ideas. Use **or** to show a choice.

    Grandpa has a lot of yard work, **and he asks** me for help.

    I want to help, **but my friends are playing** basketball.

    Should I help Grandpa, **or should I go** with my friends?

Try It

A. Choose the correct word in parentheses to join each pair of sentences. Write the new compound sentence.

1. My bicycle broke. Grandpa helped me fix it. **(and/or)** _____

_____

2. He had yard work. He spent the day with me. **(or/but)** _____

_____

3. Today I can help Grandpa. I can join my friends. **(and/or)** _____

_____

B. (4–5) Edit the paragraph. Combine two pairs of sentences with the conjunctions **and**, **but**, or **or**.

    I can play with my friends later. Grandpa needs help now. I do the right thing. Grandpa is happy for my help.

_____

_____

Use Complex Sentences

Remember: A complex sentence has an independent clause and a dependent clause.

- A **dependent clause** has a **subject** and a **verb**. It cannot stand alone as a sentence because it begins with a **subordinating conjunction**.

    because they love animals

- You can use a subordinating conjunction to join a dependent clause to an independent clause. The new sentence is a **complex sentence**.

    <u>People have</u> pets <u>**because they love** animals</u>.

    independent clause   dependent clause

- Use the subordinating conjunction **because** or **since** to tell why. Use **when** if the clauses happen at the same time. Use **before** if the dependent clause happens later. Use **after** if the dependent clause happens first.

    Ranelle has a cat **since** her apartment is small.

    She wanted a pet **when** she moved to the apartment.

    She wanted a dog **before** she moved. She got her cat **after** she moved.

Try It

A. Write a conjunction to complete each complex sentence.

1. Flash, Ranelle's cat, jumps onto the bed _____ the alarm clock rings.

2. Flash cries _____ he is hungry.

3. Ranelle feeds Flash _____ she goes to school.

B. Use a conjunction to combine each pair of sentences. Write the complex sentence.

4. Flash is waiting by the door. Ranelle comes home. _____

_____

5. Ranelle pats Flash. She puts down her backpack. _____

_____

6. Ranelle takes good care of Flash. She loves him. _____

_____

Appendix

Proofreader's Marks

Mark	Meaning	Example
∧	Add.	I am writing $\overset{an}{\wedge}$ essay.
℘	Take out.	It is i̶s̶ about friendship.
⌐	Replace with this.	I think friendship $\overset{is}{\wedge}$ if very important.
◯	Check spelling.	(Freinds) help you enjoy life.
≡	Capitalize.	m̳y̳ friends also listen to me.
/	Make lowercase.	I would do anything to help my Friends.
¶	Make new paragraph.	I know they would help me. ¶My friends are the best.

Irregular Verbs

Irregular verbs do not follow the same rules of formation as the "regular" verbs do. These verbs have special forms to show the past tense. Here are some irregular verbs.

Present	Past	Example
be	was, were	Daniel **was** sick yesterday. His brothers **were** sick, too.
become	became	I **became** angry when my sister ruined my favorite shirt.
begin	began	The parade **began** at 10 a.m.
blow	blew	The wind **blew** leaves down the street.
break	broke	Kimiko **broke** her arm when she fell off her bike.
bring	brought	We **brought** a dessert to the picnic.
build	built	The neighbors **built** a tree house in their backyard.
buy	bought	Sara **bought** a shirt in the wrong size.
catch	caught	The player **caught** the ball.
come	came	Brian **came** to the party after all.
cut	cut	My mother **cut** my hair this past weekend.
do	did	**Did** you see that accident?
draw	drew	Leon **drew** a picture of his house for the art contest.
drink	drank	I **drank** chocolate milk at lunch yesterday.
eat	ate	The teens **ate** at an Italian restaurant before the dance.
fall	fell	Mike **fell** off the ladder in the garage.
feel	felt	Carrie **felt** sad when she lost her cat.
find	found	Lanie **found** the cat in the bushes.
fly	flew	The birds **flew** south for the winter.
get	got	Monique **got** a puppy for her birthday.
give	gave	Her parents **gave** her the puppy.
grow	grew	The puppy quickly **grew** into a big dog.
go	went	We **went** to the movies yesterday night.
have	had	We **had** free tickets to the theater.
hear	heard	I **heard** a dog barking outside.
hide	hid	The frightened child **hid** under the bed.

Irregular Verbs, continued

Present	Past	Example
hit	hit	The batter **hit** a home run.
hold	held	Ellie **held** her son's hand as they crossed the street.
keep	kept	Margo **kept** a picture of her family next to her bed.
know	knew	I **knew** him in middle school.
lead	led	The conductor **led** the marching band across the field.
leave	left	He **left** his keys in the car.
make	made	My grandmother and I **made** a cherry pie yesterday.
meet	met	Juan **met** Ann at the coffee shop.
pay	paid	You **paid** too much money for that jacket.
put	put	Ahmet **put** the dishes in the cabinet.
read	read	I **read** eight books over the summer.
run	ran	Pedro **ran** the mile in six minutes.
say	said	You **said** you weren't going to the party!
see	saw	Katie **saw** several deer in the backyard.
sing	sang	Sondra **sang** the national anthem at the football game.
sit	sat	The students **sat** on the school bus.
speak	spoke	He **spoke** with his coach after practice.
stand	stood	The fans in the stadium **stood** for the national anthem.
swim	swam	The relay team **swam** back and forth across the pool.
take	took	Who **took** the last cookie?
tell	told	We **told** our parents the good news.
think	thought	I **thought** I left the keys on the table.
throw	threw	The shortstop **threw** the ball to first base.
wear	wore	Jada **wore** a costume to the Halloween party.
write	wrote	Lee **wrote** a poem for the writing contest.

Confusing Words

This section will help you choose between words that are often confused.

Confusing Word	Rule
all ready, already	Use the two-word form *all ready* to mean "completely finished." Use the one-word form *already* to mean "before." We waited an hour for dinner to be **all ready**. I'm not hungry. I **already** had dinner.
among, between	Use *among* when comparing more than two people or things. Use *between* when comparing a person or thing with one other person, thing, or group. We will split the money **among** the three of us. We will split the money **between** Sal and Jess.
amount of, number of	*Amount of* is used with nouns that cannot be counted. *Number of* is used with nouns that can be counted. The **amount of** pollution in the air is increasing. A record **number of** people attended the game.
bring, take	*Bring* means "to carry closer." *Take* means "to grasp." *Take* is often used with the preposition *away* to mean "carry away from." Please **bring** the paper to me. **Take** the book from my desk.
farther, further	*Farther* refers to a physical distance. *Further* refers to time or an amount. If you go down the road a little **farther**, you will see the sign. We will discuss this **further** after lunch.
fewer, less	*Fewer* refers to things that can be counted individually. *Less* refers to things that cannot be counted individually. The farm had **fewer** animals than the zoo. It was **less** fun to visit.

Confusing Words, continued

Confusing Word	Rule
good, well	The adjective *good* means "pleasing" or "kind." The adverb *well* means "in a good manner" or "ably." *Well* can also be used as an adjective to mean "healthy." She is a **good** person. You have performed **well**. I am glad to see that you are **well** again.
it's, its	*It's* is a contraction of *it is*. *Its* is a possessive adjective meaning "belonging to it." **It's** going to be a hot day. The dog drank all of **its** water already.
lay, lie	*Lay* means "to put in a place." It is used to describe what people do with objects. *Lie* means "to recline." People can *lie* down, but they *lay* down objects. Do not confuse this use of *lie* with the noun that means "an untruth." I **lay** the book on the table. I'm going to **lie** on the couch. If you tell a **lie**, you will be punished.
learn, teach	To *learn* is "to receive information." To *teach* is "to give information." If we want to **learn**, we have to listen. She will **teach** us how to drive.
leave, let	*Leave* means "to go away." *Let* means "to allow." **Leave** the keys on the kitchen table. I will **let** you borrow my pen.
loose, lose	*Loose* can be used as an adverb or an adjective meaning "free" or "not securely attached." The verb *lose* means "to misplace" or "not to win." The dog got **loose**, and now he is missing. Did you **lose** your homework? Did they **lose** the game by many points?

Confusing Word	Rule
raise, rise	The verb *raise* takes an object and means "to be lifted" or "to be brought up." The verb *rise* means "to lift oneself up." People can *rise*, but objects are *raised*. **Raise** the curtain for the play. She **raises** baby rabbits on her farm. I **rise** from bed at six o'clock in the morning.
real, really	*Real* means "actual." It is an adjective used to describe nouns. *Really* means "very." It is an adverb used to describe verbs, adjectives, or other adverbs. The diamond was **real**. It was not fake. The diamond was **really** beautiful.
set, sit	The verb *set* usually means "to put something down." The verb *sit* means "to go into a seated position." I **set** the box on the ground. Please **sit** while we talk.
than, then	*Than* is used to compare things. *Then* means "next" and is used to tell when something took place. She likes sweet foods more **than** salty foods. First, we will go to the grocery store. **Then** we will go home.
they're, their, there	*They're* is the contraction of *they are*. *Their* is the possessive form of the pronoun *they*. *There* is used to show a location. Peter and Ana aren't home. **They're** on vacation this week. I want to use **their** office. It is over **there**.
you're, your	*You're* is the contraction of *you are*. *Your* is a possessive adjective. It means "belonging to you." **You're** going to be late if you don't hurry. Is that **your** backpack under the couch?

Spelling Rules

Knowing spelling rules can help you when you get confused. Use these rules to help improve your spelling.

Rule	Examples
1. Always put a **u** after a **q**.	The **quick quarterback** asked **questions**. *Exceptions:* Iraq, Iraqi
2. Use **i** before **e** except after **c**.	The **fierce receiver** caught the ball. *Exceptions:* **ei**ther, h**ei**ght, th**ei**r, w**ei**rd, s**ei**ze, w**ei**gh, n**ei**ghbor
3. If a word ends in **e**, drop the **e**. Then add **-es, -ed, -er, -est,** or **-ing**.	**place + -es = places** The players took their **places** on the field. **face + -ed = faced** They **faced** their opponents. **receive + -er = receiver** The quarterback threw the ball to the **receiver**. **safe + -est = safest** It was the **safest** thing to do. **lose + -ing = losing** The team is **losing** the game.
4. If a word ends in a consonant plus **y**, change the **y** to **i**. Then add **-es, -ed, -er,** or **-est**.	**cry + -es = cries** The coach **cries** out from the sideline. **try + -ed = tried** He **tried** to help the team improve. **early + -er = earlier** He made them start practice at an **earlier** time. **lazy + -est = laziest** The team is the **laziest** team in the league.

Rule	Examples
5. For words that end in a vowel plus **y**, just add **-s** or **-ed**.	**day + -s = days** There are seven **days** in a week. **stay + -ed = stayed** The team **stayed** at practice for an extra thirty minutes.
6. If you add **-ing** to a verb that ends in **y**, do not change the **y** to **i**.	**study + ing = studying** They are **studying** videos of their games.
7. When a one-syllable word ends in one vowel and one consonant, double the final consonant before you add an ending.	**plan + n + -ed = planned** They **planned** some new plays for the next game. **big + g + -est = biggest** Then they were ready for their **biggest** challenge.